STATE OF FLUX:
Human Rights in Turkey

December 1987 Update

This report is an update to *Freedom and Fear: Human Rights in Turkey*, published by Helsinki Watch in March 1986.

36 West 44th Street
New York, NY 10036
212-840-9460

739 Eighth Street
Washington, DC 20003
202-546-9336

This report is based largely on information gathered by Jeri Laber, Executive Director of Helsinki Watch, and Lois Whitman, an attorney and consultant to the Helsinki Watch Committee, during a fact-finding mission to Turkey in June 1987. It was written by Lois Whitman and Jeri Laber.

© 1987 by the U.S. Helsinki Watch Committee
All rights reserved
Printed in the United States of America
ISBN 0-938579-68-1

HELSINKI WATCH COMMITTEE

Bound copies of this report are available for $8.00.
Previous reports on Turkey are also available:

"Violations of the Helsinki Accords: Turkey," November 1986, 91 pages, $6.00.

"Freedom and Fear: Human Rights in Turkey," March 1986, 122 pages, $6.00.

"Straws in the Wind: Prospects for Human Rights and Democracy in Turkey," July 1984, 49 pages, 6.00.

"Human Rights in Turkey's 'Transition to Democracy,'" November 1983, 117 pages, $6.00.

Table of Contents

Frequently Used Abbreviations

ANAP   Motherland Party

DISK   Confederation of Revolutionary Trade Unions

DSP   Democratic Left Party

DYP   Correct Way Party

HRA   Human Rights Association

PKK   Kurdish Workers' Party

SHP   Social Democratic Peoples' Party

TPA   Turkish Peace Association

Note: This report reflects developments in Turkey through
October 31, 1987.

INTRODUCTION

"You coined the phrase," a Turkish writer told us, "human rights in Turkey are in a 'state of flux.'" It was June 1987, and we had just arrived in Istanbul on a human rights mission; we were the fourth Helsinki Watch fact-finding delegation to visit Turkey since 1983. Our Turkish friend was referring to previous Helsinki Watch reports in which we used the phrase "state of flux" to describe the confusing, often contradictory human rights situation in Turkey since the government began its self-proclaimed return to democracy in 1983.

This report, the sixth report on human rights in Turkey that Helsinki Watch has issued since 1982, is a supplement to our March 1986 report entitled *Freedom and Fear: Human Rights in Turkey.* That report was based largely on information gathered during a Helsinki Watch fact-finding mission to Turkey in December 1985; the present report derives much of its information from our visit to Turkey in June 1987. Together with *Freedom and Fear,* it provides an overview of Turkey's human rights policies since the re-establishment of a parliament in 1983. This report also includes a long overdue addition to our previous human rights concerns in Turkey: an investigation and description of some of the human rights abuses endured by the Kurdish minority in eastern Turkey.

* * *

When a Helsinki Watch delegation first visited Turkey in September 1983 the country was under martial law, established after the September 12, 1980, military coup. We were distressed at the suppression of institutional and individual freedoms that we witnessed: all independent institutions in the country had either been taken over by the military or been banned, and private citizens who had managed to escape detention and arrest were fearful of speaking their minds to foreigners, aware that anything they said could be misconstrued by the authorities and might result in arrest and imprisonment. Their fears were well

1

founded. In the years immediately following the 1980 coup, some 178,000 Turkish citizens were detained by the police for questioning; most were brutally tortured, and many were sent to prison to await the outcome of mass trials that dragged on over a period of years. Prison conditions were deplorable, resulting in frequent hunger-strike protests by prisoners which sometimes resulted in deaths. In the early fall of 1983, the prospects for human rights in Turkey seemed ominous indeed.

When the army took control of Turkey in 1980, it brought to an end an intolerable situation of near-anarchy that had existed in the country during the late 1970s. Street violence between right and left had reached alarming proportions with many deaths each day as a result of violence. The army promised to restore order in the country, which it did, and also, eventually, to restore democracy as well. And, in its own way, it kept its promises, gradually loosening the absolute authority that it had assumed in 1980. A turning point came in November 1983 when parliamentary elections were allowed.

The November 1983 parliamentary elections were closely controlled by the military. Already banned from political life were the two mainstream parties in Turkey before the coup, as well as all former politicians. In addition, only three of the fifteen new parties that sought to participate in the elections were approved by the military. Nevertheless, the Turkish electorate found a way to voice its independence. The candidate selected and promoted by the military was resoundingly defeated, while the most independent of the three parties, the Motherland Party of Turgut Ozal, was voted into power. General Evren, who led the martial law government, continues to this day in a seven-year term as President of Turkey, having been so designated in a 1982 Constitutional referendum. But the military, since 1983, has slowly distanced itself from day-to-day rule. Martial law has been gradually lifted throughout the country, replaced by a state of emergency in many provinces which is also very strict. The lifting of martial law in Istanbul and Ankara in 1985 had a major effect on the press which is now speaking out more freely on many sensitive issues.

In December 1985, when a Helsinki Watch fact-finding mission returned to Turkey, the situation was dramatically different from 1983, especially with regard to the parliament and the press, a change which continues to the present time. The existence of a parliament with representatives who are responsible to an electorate has led to open parliamentary debate on some of the most delicate human rights issues, including the continued use of torture in police detention centers and the deplorable conditions in Turkish prisons. A parliamentary commission conducted an investigation of prison conditions in 1985 and issued a report with some pointed recommendations. The opposition parties in the Turkish parliament have taken up the cause of human rights, constantly attacking the government on this issue, and their criticisms receive extensive coverage in the press. For a while in 1985 and 1986, the issue of torture seemed to consume the country; each day brought new reports from victims, culminating in a sensational expose by a former policeman/torturer who described instances and techniques of torture in a graphically illustrated series in the press. Yet all the investigations and incriminations had little effect on actual practices: we have received ample evidence that torture is continuing unabated and that conditions in the prisons remain unchanged.

In our March 1986 report entitled *Freedom and Fear: Human Rights in Turkey*, we concluded that Turkey is "a society in ferment, its direction uncharted." Nevertheless, we remained optimistic: "That very ferment is the best reason for hope."

Unfortunately, our expectations for continued human rights progress in Turkey have not yet been fulfilled. We determined during our most recent visit, in June 1987, that human rights in Turkey are still in a state of flux. Positive steps are continually being undermined by negative actions. Although there have been some noteworthy improvements, mainly in the area of freedom of association, the continued use of torture in police detention is both distressing and inexplicable, given the Turkish authorities' claims that they have brought an end to the use of torture and that any incidents that come to light are either fabrications aimed at influencing world opinion against Turkey or are isolated cases of police brutality. The evidence of torture that we received indicates that torture is still routinely practiced in Turkey, involving the same techniques in the same police stations as has been documented in the past. If there are fewer instances of torture in Turkey today, it is because there are fewer arrests than before, and not because practices have noticeably changed.

3

On the positive side, there is now a Human Rights Association in Turkey that has received official permission to function and is conducting investigations and issuing reports on many human rights violations in the country. There is also an Association of Families of Detainees and Convicts, which is tolerated by the authorities; we attended a public meeting organized by the group in Istanbul at which repressive prison conditions were openly discussed and deplored. Yet (and there is always a "yet" when discussing human rights improvements in Turkey) other organizations have been denied the right to function: a group called Physicians for the Prevention of Nuclear War was banned two weeks after it was formed and a case was opened against 49 of its founders; an Association for the Purification of the Turkish Language was also closed down.

In similar fashion, the press remains outspoken in its criticisms of human rights violations in Turkey and has even begun to speak tentatively about a subject that has traditionally been forbidden: the situation of the Kurds in eastern Turkey. But journalists and editors proceed at some risk: they are frequently brought to court for articles that they have written, and magazines with controversial articles have been banned or seized from the newsstands. A large number of books and publications are officially banned in Turkey.

The Turkish government, ever mindful of world opinion and particularly solicitous of Western Europe since its recent bid for full membership in the European Community, has agreed to the right of individual petition to the European Commission of Human Rights. This is potentially a most significant human rights advance for Turkish citizens, who now have the right to file their individual complaints with the Commission. But the Turkish government has qualified its acceptance of the right of individual petition in various ways, and it remains to be seen how the complaint procedure will work in practice.

The basic problem with regard to human rights in Turkey remains unchanged. It stems from the repressive 1982 Constitution and a series of equally repressive laws that remain in force, exerting a chilling effect on the society. Many of the freedoms that have been tolerated in Turkey since 1983 may very well be a gesture by the government to international opinion, rather than the

4

reflection of a genuine desire for democracy and human rights. And because these freedoms have no legal guarantees, they can be easily reversed if there is a change of policy. Unless the restrictive legislation in Turkey is changed, any human rights progress may turn out to be transitory.

* * *

During its 1985 mission to Turkey, Helsinki Watch received unprecedented cooperation from the Turkish government and met with many Turkish officials. We were gratified by the government's cooperation and by the opportunity it provided for us to conduct detailed and frank conversations with officials in the various ministries about human rights policies and practices in Turkey. We also saw this openness on the part of the government as a positive indication of change in its attitude toward human rights organizations and their concerns.

The Turkish government's attitude toward Helsinki Watch was very different, however, with regard to our most recent mission in June 1987. When the authorities discovered that we planned to enlarge our previous agenda to include an investigation of the situation of the Kurdish minority in southeastern Turkey, doors that had previously been opened to us were closed. We were told, in advance of our trip, that not only would we be denied meetings with officials in southeastern Turkey, but that officials in Ankara would also be unwilling to see us. Prime Minister Ozal recently stated at a public meeting that Helsinki Watch tended to talk to the wrong people and thus get a mistaken idea of what is going on in the country. Yet the government's refusal to meet with us, short of a few perfunctory meetings with spokespeople in the Foreign Ministry, made it impossible for us to receive first hand explanations of the government's point of view.

Turkish officials, it appears, are unhappy with the fact that Helsinki Watch, after hearing the official point of view in 1985, has continued to criticize many of Turkey's human rights practices. They were particularly upset at our decision to investigate the situation of the Kurds, the most sensitive human rights issue in Turkey.

5

We traveled to eastern Turkey despite the government's disapproval. No efforts were made to prevent us from going there or to limit our activities while we were there. We were able to talk with a number of Kurdish people-- lawyers, political leaders, journalists, businessmen--who described a situation of extreme repression that has continued to worsen in many respects since the 1980 coup. The situation is complicated by guerrilla warfare that has been raging in the border areas since 1984, waged by Kurdish terrorists seeking an independent Kurdistan.

The Kurdish minority in Turkey has long been denied any semblance of ethnic identity: the Kurdish language, culture, customs and history are not recognized by the Turkish government which denies the very existence of the Kurds. Recent military actions in the area appear to have given the government license for still greater intimidation of the Kurds. Ordinary citizens are caught between the army and the guerrillas and are being persecuted by both. The guerrillas, a relatively small band according to the Turkish government, have been ruthless in their attacks against innocent civilians, including many women and children. On the other hand, however, the Turkish army seems to be waging warfare against the Kurdish population as a whole, accusing the local people of assisting the terrorists. Some parts of the southeast that we visited seemed to be in a continual state of seige. We received more complaints about the day-to-day practices of the army than we did about sporadic attacks by the guerrillas.

Even on the basis of a cursory inspection, it seemed clear to us that the Turkish government is pursuing a self-destructive policy in the east. By refusing to recognize the ethnic rights and economic needs of the local population, the government is fanning flames of hatred and revolt and encouraging the Kurds to identify their own well-being with the aims of the secessionist guerrillas. Although most Kurds reportedly reject the terrorist tactics of the guerrillas and do not wish to secede from Turkey, the government is not providing them with a feasible alternative. "We don't like the terrorists," we were told by some local Kurds, "but they are the best we have right now." And a parliamentarian from the area told us that support for the guerrillas has increased from zero to 40 percent in his province because of the strong-arm tactics of the Turkish army

6

and the government. "The people don't want a separate Kurdistan," this politician assured us, "they want freedom."

*   *   *

The human rights situation in Turkey remains in a state of flux, but there are still good reasons for optimism. A number of important steps have already been taken by the government to improve the situation and a verbal commitment to human rights and democracy has been publicly made by most of the major political forces in the country. Despite its defensive posture with regard to the most recent Helsinki Watch fact-finding mission, Turkey has proved to be responsive to international criticisms of its human rights practices; it is therefore important that Western governments and international human rights organizations continue to keep up the pressure for change.

Most important of all is the will of the Turkish people themselves: during successive trips to Turkey, we have become increasingly impressed by their dedication and their strong desire for independence and democracy. This provides a basis for our continued hope that Turkey will ultimately achieve a government that respects human rights in its actions as well as in its words and provides guarantees for their protection.

Jeri Laber
Lois Whitman

December 1987

I. LEGAL SAFEGUARDS

Previous Helsinki Watch reports have described Turkey's repressive Constitution, passed in 1982, and a number of restrictive laws that severely hamper freedom and human rights in Turkey. Since the last Helsinki Watch fact-finding mission in December 1985, however, martial law has gradually been ended in all of Turkey's 67 provinces, the last four, Hakkari, Mardin, Siirt and Diyarbakir, in eastern Turkey in July 1987. Nevertheless, a state of emergency still exists in nine provinces under which individual liberties can be sharply curtailed. In addition, in July 1987, a special governor was appointed to oversee the eight eastern provinces--Diyarbakir, Mardin, Tunceli, Hakkari, Siirt, Van, Bingol and Elazig--where Kurdish guerrillas have been active, and the governor has been given extra powers to bring the area under control.

In addition to the ending of martial law, there have been a few constructive legal changes. A law for reduction of sentences was passed in March 1986 and resulted in the release of 31,000 prisoners, according to the European Commission on Human Rights (see *Political Prisoners*). In April 1987 the Parliament abolished the law on internal exile, a law which permitted the courts to impose a sentence of internal exile to follow the completion of a prison sentence.

In January 1987, the Turkish government recognized the right of individual petition to the European Commission of Human Rights. Unfortunately, however, the government has qualified its recognition in a number of ways, including stating that the "notion of a 'democratic society' in ... the [European] Convention [on Human Rights] must be understood in conformity with the principles laid down in the Turkish Constitution and in particular its Preamble and its Article 13." The Preamble and Article 13 set forth a number of restrictions on fundamental rights and freedoms of the Turkish people. The Preamble says, for example:

. . . no protection shall be afforded to thoughts or opinions contrary to Turkish national interests, the principle of the existence of Turkey as an indivisible entity with its state and territory, Turkish historical and moral values, or the nationalism, principles, reforms and modernism of Ataturk. . .

Article 13 says:

Fundamental rights and freedoms may be restricted by law, in conformity with the letter and spirit of the Constitution, with the aim of safeguarding the indivisible integrity of the State with its territory and nation, national sovereignty, the Republic, national security, public order, general peace, the public interest, public morals and public health, and also for specific reasons set forth in the relevant articles of the Constitution...

In addition, the government restricted the right of petition to allegations concerning acts or omissions of public authorities inside of Turkey, thus denying to Turks living abroad access to the Commission. Cases involving military personnel or actions taken under a state of emergency or martial law were also excluded by the government. (See Appendix 1.) The government's conditional acceptance of the right of individual appeal has been challenged by four countries that have also signed the European Convention on Human Rights--Sweden, Norway, Luxembourg and Greece. The matter will be tested when an individual complaint reaches the Commission. *Yeni Gundem*, an Istanbul weekly, reported in March that Hasan Basri Aydin had filed a complaint with the Commission alleging improper denial of a passport.

The 1982 Constitution remains in effect in Turkey, and with it restrictive laws concerning freedom of speech and association, political freedom and rights of political and other prisoners to due process of law. According to Teoman Evren, president of the Union of Turkish Bar Associations, Turkey's legal structure--the Constitution as well as current criminal laws--may infringe on human rights and cause problems. As an example, he cited the police law and the widening of police powers. "By law," Mr. Evren said, "only a judge can order a search; however, in cases of danger or necessity, the prosecutor can order a search, and, in cases of immediate danger, the police can order a search. If you consider everything an emergency, any search can take place."

Turgut Kazan, a prominent Istanbul attorney, has frequently criticized the 1982 Constitution. In an interview with us in Istanbul in June 1987, he elaborated: "The usual Constitution defends the rights of citizens against the state; ours describes the power of the state against the individual." He quoted a professor of his who refers to the present Constitution as an "anti-Constitution," and believes that no Constitution would be preferable: "People would then be able to exert some rights, based on international examples." Mr. Kazan told us that Turkey's "awful Constitution" is surpassed by laws that are still worse-- for example, laws on meetings and associations, collective bargaining and strikes and lock-outs, higher education and political parties. "All," he said, "sharply restrict the rights of Turkish citizens."

Opposition parties within the Parliament have prepared legislation to correct some of the current inequities. Bulent Ecevit, a former prime minister who until recently was banned from political activity by Provisional Article 4 of the Constitution, told us that the Democratic Left Party (DSP) will reintroduce a bill to allow detainees to talk with their lawyers at any time after they are detained (a similar bill was defeated in Parliament in 1986.) In addition, the DSP will introduce bills to lift the death penalty, to restrict security investigations to people applying for high security jobs, to restore the right of citizenship to over 8,000 Turks living abroad who have been deprived of Turkish citizenship, and to prevent the withholding of passports without a court decision.

Erdal Inonu, a former professor who heads the Social Democratic People's Party (SHP), told us in June 1987 that the SHP had proposed similar bills to improve human rights: the SHP sponsored the bill to provide immediate access to an attorney which was defeated in Parliament in 1986. Other legislaion--for example, a law providing general amnesty for political prisoners--died in committee.

When we asked Bulent Akarcali, deputy chairman of the ruling Motherland Party (ANAP), why his party had defeated the bill for immediate access to an attorney, he said that the introduction of the bill was politically motivated, and that it was not possible to change one part of the criminal pro-

11

cedure law without changing the entire system. Akarcali went on to point out that the present law was a necessary part of a framework that was established to end the anarchy which had prevailed in Turkey before the 1980 coup.

Turkey's current penal code, which is based on the Italian penal code enacted under Mussolini, has been widely criticized as repressive and in need of modernization. A proposed new penal code drafted by a commission headed by Prof. Sulhi Donmezer of Istanbul University, however, apparently contains elements that are even more repressive than the original. According to *The Economist* of November 1, 1986, the most controversial articles in the existing penal code--articles 140, 141, 142 and 163--have been retained. These articles forbid engaging in communist or separatist organizations or propaganda or advocating a non-secular state. A new offense of "praising religious governments" has been added, and sentences for inflicting torture are *reduced* to a maximum of 12 years from a maximum of 20.

According to *Ozgurluge*, March-May 1986, the Ankara Bar Association raised the following issues in a statement to the press after the draft penal code was released in February 1987:

"Crimes of thought" have been carried over into the new draft, with even a broader range of applications;

Clauses that define "propaganda and organizing against the present political order of the state" as criminal abridge in great measure the freedom of political criticism and the expression of the free will of individuals and groups, and are unthinkable in democracies;

"Crimes against the state" have also been carried over, and their range broadened, the only exception being those articles under which the extreme rightist militia men have been brought to trial, which now call for reduced sentences;

Under Article 316, on "violating the constitution," the element of "force (violence)" has been stricken from the text of the parent article (146 in the old Penal Code) and "unconstitutional means" (of changing the government) has been substituted instead. Moreover, the sentences to be asked for lesser accomplices in such crimes have been substantially increased. In this section, new categories have been created such as "detrimental to national interest," or "undermining national sentiments," which are wide open to interpretation;

Big reductions (up to 7/8) in the sentences of those defendants who agree to turn informant open the way for incitement to criminal actions through the use of *agents provocateurs*;

The introduction of the concept of "crimes against religions under the guarantee of the constitution" violates the principle of laicism, on which the Turkish Republic is based.

The statement of the Ankara Bar Association concludes: "In brief, the social equilibrium which should be achieved within a democratic system, has been attempted to be instituted through criminal sanctions, while not one step has been taken in the direction of a democratic state respectful of the supremacy of law."

Teoman Evren, president of the Union of Turkish Bar Associations, told us that the proposed code had good and bad elements; on the one hand, he said, there was a lessening in the number of laws and in the sentences for crimes against property. For crimes against the state, however, and against national security, there was little or no reduction in sentences.

A number of attorneys and others have raised serious questions about the proposed code. Turgut Kazan told us that the proposed code not only retains all the political crimes mentioned in the present penal code but adds some additional political crimes that are even more vague and restrictive. He pointed as an example to a provision that sets heavy penalties for people who spread information that damages the economy of the country. Mr. Kazan said: "You could be guilty of this crime if you said 'the crops are bad this year.'"

Nuri Colakoglu, a senior news editor of the newspaper *Milliyet*, told us that the draft of the new penal code had been greeted with indignation by many and might not become law.

Because no one in the Ministry of Justice was willing to meet with us, we were unable to discuss the government's position on the proposed code. In

February, however, *Cumhuriyet* quoted Minister of Justice Oltan Sungurlu: "Our stance on this issue (Articles 141, 142, and 163 of the present Code, involving 'crimes of thought') is perfectly clear. No, we are not doing away with these articles. We support them." *Nokta* reported on April 26, 1987, that Minister Sungurlu had declared that "unconstitutional means of overthrowing a government," for which a death penalty may be asked under the new draft (Article 318), could include, for example, calls for a general strike.

In addition to pointing out problems in the Constitution and legal framework, and in the proposed new penal code, several lawyers with whom we spoke criticized the judiciary, saying that there had been no independent judiciary since the 1980 coup, since the judiciary is under the control of the executive department. Others, however, seemed to believe that some judges were able to maintain a fair degree of independence within the restrictive framework in which they work.

Many Turks believe that it is almost impossible for a defendant accused of a political crime to receive a fair trial. This view has been supported by outside international groups. In an extensive report in October 1986, *Unfair Trial of Political Prisoners in Turkey*, Amnesty International concluded:

> Military courts are not independent from the executive authorities, either in law or in practice.

> Lawyers defending political prisoners have been harassed and impeded in many ways, in particular by insufficient access to their clients and the denial of private conversations.

> Detainees charged with political offences have been subjected to excessively long trials and periods of pre-trial detention, amounting to more than five years in many cases.

> Military courts trying political prisoners have repeatedly failed to investigate allegations by defendants that statements had been extracted under torture.

> More than 48,000 political prisoners tried by military courts since the first declaration of martial law in December 1978

14

have therefore been sentenced to imprisonment or the death penalty after an unfair trial.

Although martial law has now been limited to five provinces, military courts in provinces previously under martial law continue to function and at least 800 cases remain pending before them.

Many lawyers with whom we spoke in June agreed with Amnesty's conclusions. Lawyers were particularly upset by their inability to give what they considered to be adequate representation to their clients, particularly those accused of political offenses. According to Teoman Evren, president of the Union of Turkish Bar Associations, "Lawyers can't see their clients while the indictment is being drawn up and the investigation is continuing--everything is secret, and the defendant remains without a defense. The problem of access to defendants is particularly severe in military courts, and the military court has the authority to throw the lawyer out--a gross infringement of the right to defense. Also, evidence against a defendant is kept secret--even those types of evidence which are available to a lawyer in a civilian court are kept secret from a lawyer in a martial law court, for example reports of experts, doctors' reports and the testimony of the defendant." Mr. Evren was also disturbed by a provision of the law that permits convicted prisoners to be taken out of prison and back to the police station for further investigation.

A prominent lawyer spoke along similar lines: "There is no such thing as a right to a defense in Turkey now. According to the state of emergency law, the maximum period of detention is 30 days--15 days that can be doubled with the approval of the governor. But what happens is that a detainee will be taken somewhere--no one knows where, no one knows what happened, no one can intervene. The person who's being held can't see a lawyer, and the lawyer can't go there to intervene, even though today torture in all forms and techniques is still going on. After thirty days without an attorney the right to defense is dead. A trial after thirty days of incommunicado detention is a comedy. And the final verdict is based on what the defendant said during those thirty days--the 'confession' is the main evidence brought against a defendant.

15

"You can only see your client after the preliminary investigation is over," he went on, "and after the client has been formally arrested. When I get calls from the family of someone who has been detained but not formally arrested, my heart hurts--it's so difficult for a lawyer to have to say 'there's nothing I can do.'" Asked what would happen if a lawyer went, for example, to the police interrogation center at Gayrettepe and asked to see his client, this lawyer laughed; "You see it in American films," he said, "but it's impossible in Turkey."

Lawyers who represent clients in southeastern Turkey--the Kurdish areas--have an even more difficult job. One lawyer who has represented many defendants incarcerated in Diyarbakir Prison said: "Many of my clients are ignorant peasants, Kurds who have been detained because they are thought to be helping the PKK [Kurdish Workers' Party--a militant separatist organization carrying on guerrilla warfare in the southeast--see section on *The Kurdish Minority*]. Most of them don't speak Turkish, only Kurdish--but I'm not allowed to speak Kurdish with them in prison. As a result, I can't communicate at all--I can't get a client's proofs, his history, his experience; I can't represent him at all--it's a farce. Even with those clients who speak Turkish, you can't really talk with them. You meet with them in a room with iron bars and grills with tiny holes--you can't even see their faces. Two soldiers stand near the prisoner, and one soldier near the lawyer--all of them listen to your conversation. There have been cases where what a client told his lawyer was used against him in court."

A former prisoner who spent many years in Diyarbakir Prison told us that it had been easy for prisoners to contact their lawyers before the 1980 coup. "But after that there was always a soldier with my lawyer and me who would listen in on our conversation. Prison officials told us, 'Don't speak too long with your lawyer; as soon as the private hits your leg, get up and leave.' Sometimes I had half a minute, or a minute, with my lawyer, sometimes as long as two minutes--that's all."

Several lawyers told us that lawyers had been harassed and prevented from providing an adequate defense for clients under martial law, but that since the end of martial law, fewer obstacles were placed in the way of representing clients. A lawyer in Tunceli in southeastern Turkey said, however: "In the east, the tolerance for a lawyer to practice his profession is very small." Lawyers in

Diyarbakir gave us the names of four lawyers who had been imprisoned for their actions in defending their clients--all have been released and are now living in Europe.

None of the lawyers with whom we met knew of any lawyers now serving time in prison for defending their clients. But as recently as 1985 four other attorneys were sentenced to a year in prison for stating in court that the judges had not taken seriously their clients' allegations of torture in prison. Ultimately the military court of appeals overturned their sentences.

Two other recent cases have been reported in the press:

- In September, a 79-year-old lawyer, Saffet Nezihi Bolukbasi, was sentenced to six months in prison for criticizing in court a decision of the Court of Cassations, saying: "The contradiction in the decision exceeds logic and brings chaos to law; it is an anomaly and needs to be corrected." Because of his age, the tribunal commuted the sentence to a fine. Mr. Bolukbasi is well known in Turkey as the attorney for the poet Nazim Hikmet. *Nokta*, Sept. 21, 1986.
- Writer Aziz Nesin petitioned an Ankara civil court to open a lawsuit against President Evren for defamation, for accusing the signers of an intellectuals' petition of treason. The court rejected the petition. The public prosecutor then brought charges against Nesin's lawyer, Emin Deger, for "insulting the president" in his petition. *Cumhuriyet*, March 2, 1987.

Some lawyers in Diyarbakir continue to be harassed; one told us he had been warned by the head of the gendarmerie (security forces) not to pursue his cases so aggressively. The commander told him: "Stop following your cases, or I will follow you. I might kill you." The lawyer told him that it was his profession, and that he would continue to do his job. He believes that he is followed and his actions watched; his office has been searched. He asked us not to use his name or send him mail.

Another lawyer who had met with an international group that visited Diyarbakir told us that the security forces called him in after the meeting to ask him what had been discussed.

A former Diyarbakir Prison inmate told us that he had known lawyers imprisoned in Diyarbakir who got in trouble with prison guards because they complained in court about mistreatment in prison. One of these, Huseyin Yildirim, was stripped naked and pulled around by a rope tied to his penis.

The same former prisoner told us that prison officials had tortured him by beating him and leaving him in a cell full of excrement in order to make him sign a statement saying that his lawyer was representing him without pay for political reasons--a statement that was untrue.

Many lawyers in Turkey, despite harassment and abuse, continue to represent political defendants to the best of their ability--sometimes at great personal risk. These courageous lawyers often put their lives on the line to try to protect their clients. Teomen Evren, president of the Union of Turkish Bar Associations, said: "I'm proud of the behavior of lawyers in Turkey--they make sure no one remains without a defense in Turkey. And they make their views known in the press and in legal societies." An Istanbul lawyer told us that in June the Istanbul Bar Association convened a special meeting to protest a ruling by the Minister of Justice against two lawyers who had complained about a judge to the judges' council. The president of the association, Selahattin Sulhi Tekin, was quoted in *Cumhuriyet* on June 14, 1987, as saying: "This incident concerns all of our colleagues across Turkey. If the right to defend is under pressure, court decisions cannot be just. We are going to fight until the Minister of Justice apologizes."

II. FUNDAMENTAL RIGHTS AND FREEDOMS

Freedom of Speech

The return to parliamentary government in Turkey in 1983 and the gradual lifting of martial law has resulted in greater freedom of speech over the past few years. People who were afraid to speak openly, or for quotation, prior to 1983 are now speaking freely about human rights problems in Turkey. Of the people we interviewed in June 1987, many were willing to be quoted and assured us that we could use their names. There are still forbidden topics, however: those who spoke to us about the treatment of the Kurds in eastern Turkey, for example, and fundamentalist Moslems who are seeking greater religious freedom, stipulated that their remarks were strictly off-the-record.

Newspapers now quite openly criticize the government, but not President Evren or the military (see *Freedom of the Press*). Politicians also openly criticize the government; former prime ministers Bulent Ecevit and Suleyman Demirel spoke candidly to us about what they consider improper actions of the government (see *Political Freedom*). But they, too, are taking risks: newspaper reporters are sometimes investigated, prosecuted and sentenced for their writings, and former politicians have been prosecuted for making political speeches. Turkish Radio and Television (TRT) remains under the exclusive control of the government (see *Political Freedom*).

The potential consequences of speaking out publicly were demonstrated on November 12, 1986, when three men were arrested for taking part in a July 26 panel discussion sponsored by the journal *Sacak*. The subject of the discussion, which took place in an Ankara movie house and was attended by 800 or 900 people, was "Intra-Party Democracy in Socialist Parties"; the panelists discussed internal democracy within a theoretical Socialist Party. The three men spent three months in Ankara Prison and were released on February 13, 1987. Their trial before the State Security Court began in February and is continuing.

We met with the three men in Ankara in June--Halil Berktay, former-ly an instructor at the University of Ankara, now a journalist; Ali Kalan, a lawyer; and Cenan Bicakci, a former union organizer who now owns a small art gallery. A fourth panelist, Sungur Savran, an economist, formerly an instructor at the University of Istanbul, was also charged, but was abroad.

The panelists told us that the case was "absurd to begin with." They were charged, under Article 142, clause 1 of the penal code, with Communist propaganda, which carries a sentence of from 5 to 12 years. They said that the discussion had nothing to do with establishing a Communist Party or with over-throwing the government by force. The panel discussion was taped by police, a standard practice, and the tape was then given to an associate professor of criminal law at the Law Faculty of Ankara University, who judged the text to be a violation of Article 142. On that basis, the prosecution started proceedings. All three panelists emphasized that they were not discussing how a Socialist Party might come to power or what its program or statutes would be, but rather the question of what kind of internal democracy such a party should have. They consider their case a "crime of conscience," dealing only with their freedom to think and express their convictions. Despite this, they were not sure of the out-come of the case.

Freedom of the Press

The legal restrictions on press freedom that we noted in previous Hel-sinki Watch reports continue today. The Constitution forbids anyone to write or print "any news or articles which threaten the internal or external security of the State or ... which tend to incite offense, riot or insurrection ..." A restric-tive press law can be used to prosecute journalists. Under Article 140 of the penal code a person can be sent to prison for writing or saying things that damage Turkey's reputation abroad.

Despite these legal limitations, Turkish journalists have been criticiz-ing many aspects of the government and publishing articles on subjects that were taboo only a short while ago. Bulent Akarcali, deputy chairman of the ruling Motherland Party, affirming that freedom of information is the most important protection for human rights, told us in a June 1987 interview that the Turkish

20

press is free to write anything and that there is no human rights issue that cannot be aired in print. Mr. Akarcali believes that the Turkish press is freer than the press in the United States because the Turkish press can't be sued for libel. There is also a wider range of left-wing publications today than was permissible a few years ago.

Hasan Cemal, the editor of *Cumhuriyet* and the author of two recent books on freedom of the press during military rule, also described greater press freedom. He characterized the press as "very lively since martial law was lifted in Istanbul in November 1985." Mr. Cemal no longer receives calls from the military about what can or cannot be published. The press freely criticizes Prime Minister Ozal and members of his government, sometimes in vitriolic terms, but it is still not feasible to criticize President Evren or the military, and several cases are pending against journalists who have done so.

Nuri Colakoglu of *Milliyet* told us that journalists now are less intimidated and feel freer to write. He said that journalists would have gone to prison three or four years ago for articles that are now being published. As an example, he described *Milliyet*'s plans to publish interviews with members of the illegal Turkish Communist Party now living in Germany and England. Mr. Colakoglu also gave an example of the government's contradictory policies: *Milliyet* published a series of articles about Turks who had been deprived of their citizenship while living abroad, describing how those who receive warrants from the military and do not return within 15 days lose their citizenship and passports. Following the publication of the *Milliyet* articles, a government minister said that these cases might be taken up again and that an amnesty might be issued. The two *Milliyet* writers of the series, however, were prosecuted.

The situation of the Kurds in eastern Turkey has long been taboo. Until very recently, the word "Kurd" itself was never used to describe Kurds in eastern Turkey; newspapers might refer to the "situation in the east," or to "separatists," or "mountain Turks," but never to "Kurds." Early in 1987, however, a *Milliyet* reporter wrote that there is a problem in Turkey that must be discussed, and that it first had to be named--"the Kurdish problem." No legal action was taken against the writer or the newspaper, and since that time Turkish newspapers and magazines have begun using the word "Kurd." On June 22,

1987, Hasan Cemal, in a *Cumhuriyet* editorial on terrorist activities in the southeast, said:

> We have to live with this problem until we totally understand it and establish the ways to resolve it. But what is it? Of course, the word "Kurdish" has to be used in identifying the problem. ... The extremely poor socioeconomic conditions in southeastern Turkey must be corrected and the habit of turning a blind eye to the communal and cultural characteristics of the people in that region must be halted as well.

On July 10, 1987, *Milliyet*, continuing this trend, published an article by Professor Mumtaz Soysal declaring that it was "a national right for people to speak their mother tongue," an obvious reference to the Kurds. The article was followed by a column in *Milliyet* by M. Ali Birand on July 21, 1987, entitled, "Let's take a different approach toward the question of the Kurds."

In August 1987, however, a Turkish court banned an issue of *2000'e Dogru*, an Istanbul weekly, before it went to the newsstands, because it contained two articles on the Kurds. The grounds were that it "openly incited people to hatred and animosity against authorities by emphasizing ethnic differences." One of the articles quoted Kemal Ataturk on the Kurdish issue and contained archive documents showing that Ataturk once promised autonomy to the Kurds. The other article was written by a former politician living in southeast Turkey; it advocated equal rights for the Kurds. According to a Turkish reporter, this is the first time the government has stepped in to ban a publication before it has been distributed. The magazine published a new version a few days later, leaving four censored pages blank. The public prosecutor has begun an investigation.

On September 23, another issue of *2000'e Dogru* was confiscated, this time after it had appeared on the newsstands. The issue contained an article quoting Kemal Ataturk as saying: "It [is] necessary to establish an autonomous regime in the Kurdish dominated regions in accordance with Turkey's foreign policy and political beliefs." The issue was seized because the article was found harmful because it "weaken[ed] national feelings." An issue of *Yeni Gundem* that was devoted to the Kurdish question was also confiscated from the newsstands.

A journalist whom we interviewed in June pointed out that what is written about the Kurds is often slanted, that newspapers present an inaccurate picture of events in the east, and that journalists continue to censor themselves, an issue "too delicate to discuss with other reporters, only with good friends." Another reporter whom we interviewed criticized colleagues in the press for not discussing issues candidly, and believes that the press, with some exceptions, is not courageous in trying to expand the limits on press freedom.

Many reporters and editors of newspapers and magazines have been investigated, prosecuted and occasionally sentenced for what they have written and published. Although most are acquitted after living through cases that drag on for months, such prosecutions clearly exert a chilling effect.

In March 1986 an obscenity law, the Law to Protect Minors, went into effect. This law has apparently been used frequently against magazines and against writers and publishers of books, and less often against newspapers. *Cumhuriyet* reported in February 1987 that 57 legal proceedings had been brought against five daily papers and twelve weekly or monthly magazines for "harmful articles" using this law.

The following cases, selected from the many reports we have received, indicate some of the problems faced by the press:

- In July 1986 two journalists of the weekly *Hafta Sonu*, Huseyin Olcay and Vedat Levent Aras, were sentenced to three years in prison for having criticized the Ministry of Communications.
- In September 1986 Okay Gonensin was tried and acquitted for having referred to the "Council for the Protection of Minors from Harmful Publications" as the "Harmful Council."
- In September 1986 the weekly *Karacadag* was closed down indefinitely for publishing an article about torture of villagers in the east carried out by the commander of a gendarmerie unit.
- In November 1986 two journalists of the daily *Hergun*, Veysi Sozuer and Mustafa Karapinar, were sentenced to 10-month prison terms for having insulted the government in an article published in 1978.

- In December 1986 Abdullah Inal, a *Milliyet* correspondent in Antalya, was arrested and imprisoned for insulting the mayor of Antalya.
- In December 1986 Cuneyt Arcayurek was tried for a May 1986 series of articles, "Five Minutes to Democracy," that appeared in *Cumhuriyet*.
- In March 1987 Ilhan Selcuk, a columnist, and Okay Gonensin, the managing editor of *Cumhuriyet*, were tried for a December 1986 column which purportedly insulted the members of the National Security Council.
- Issues of the monthlies *Yeni Cozum* and *Cagdas Yol* were confiscated in March 1987.
- In April 1987 two cases were brought against the weekly *2000'e Dogru* for articles insulting President Evren and insulting "the revered memory of Kemal Ataturk." In July Fatma Yazici, the editor of *2000'e Dogru*, was sentenced to one year and four months for the article that "defamed" President Evren.
- Seven cases are pending against the weekly *Yeni Gundem* for an issue on homosexuals deemed harmful, an article about terrorist activities in the east, and other articles, some dealing with the Kurds. An eighth case concerned an article about the late film director Yilmaz Guney. The editor of *Yeni Gundem* was acquitted of that charge in July 1987.
- Two cartoonists and the former editor of the weekly humor magazine *Limon* were sentenced to three months or fined in Istanbul on July 9, 1987, for publishing "insulting" cartoons about Prime Minister Ozal.

A number of journalists, most of them arrested right after the 1980 coup for journalistic activities predating the military takeover, are serving sentences--some extremely long--in Turkish prisons. We were not able to determine the exact number. Amnesty International has information about 10 journalists; Hasan Cemal of *Cumhuriyet* told us there were 17 people in prison who were called journalists, of which the Turkish Journalists' Asso ciation considers only three to be real journalists, as the other 14 are former editors of extremist publications. In March 1987 the Ankara-based Contemporary

24

Journalists' Association published a list of 13 journalists still in prison--12 in Cannakale and one in Bursa.

The editor of a publication may be sentenced to seven years for each article in the publication, which leads to some very long prison sentences. A journalist, Erhan Tuskan, charged under Article 142 of the Turkish penal code with Communist propaganda, is serving a sentence of 48 years and 10 months in Canakkale E-type prison. Another, Candemir Ozler, is serving 23 years and 10 months in Canakkale for articles published in the journal *Savas Yolu*.

Freedom to Publish

There is no pre-censorship of publishers in Turkey. Nuri Colakoglu of *Milliyet* told us that no one is stopped from writing or publishing, but "you don't know where the lightning will strike." Lightning has struck a number of books on sexuality, as well as novels considered to have obscene passages. In October 1986 a book called *Homosexuality of Yesterday and Today in Turkey*, by Dr. Arslan Yuzgun, was declared harmful by the Council for the Protection of Minors. Dr. Haydar Dumen's book, *Sexual Problems*, was confiscated after a trial in March 1987; an earlier book of Dr. Dumen's, *Sexual Life II*, was acquitted of charges of obscenity in December 1986.

In April 1987 Fusun Erbulak's novel, *Spiral*, was found harmful by the Court of Cassations (an appellate court); however the court overturned prison sentences for Erbulak and her publisher, Ramazan Yasar, saying such crimes were no longer punishable by prison sentences. In July 1986 Ahmet Altan and his publisher Erdal Oz were tried for obscenity for the novel *The Trace in the Water*.

Pinar Kur, a popular novelist, has seen three of her books banned--the first by the military, the others by the Council to Protect Minors. In a June 1987 interview, Ms. Kur told us that her latest book, *Unending Love*, was banned in December 1986 for what the Council considered obscene descriptions of love-making. The Council, as quoted by *Cumhuriyet* on December 17, 1986, said that Ms. Kur's novel "would corrupt minors by causing them to misunderstand the contemporary era, rendering them daydreamers." The Council also said that "a literary novel should not contradict the value systems of the society; it should

25

not have slang or obscene language." A trial was held in April 1987; no decision has been reached yet. Ms. Kur's earlier book, *A Woman to be Hanged*, was banned after it was made into a film, even though the book had been published eight years earlier. The banning of the film was reversed on appeal but the book is still banned. Kur now supports herself by writing articles. She told us that she had started working on a new novel, but gave it up, asking herself, "Who am I writing for, the censors? What's the point?" She observed sadly, "I am free, but my novels are in prison."

The banning of books appears to be systematic and thorough; in October 1986, the Ministry of Justice published a detailed list of the titles of publications banned up to that time and publications that are banned from entry into Turkey by government decrees. The list was sent to the political sections of local prefectures and to the directors of educational institutions, according to *Info-Turk*, October 1986.

In February 1987 *Cumhuriyet* reported that criminal proceedings had been brought against the writers, translators and publishers of 240 publications within the previous three and a half years, as a result of orders issued by two Istanbul district courts and the Istanbul State Security Court. On December 18, 1986, 39 tons of books, periodicals and newspapers were sent to the SEKA paper mill to be pulped. According to the February 19, 1987, *Cumhuriyet*, among the pulped publications were Penguin's *Map of the World* and *Map of Europe*, *National Geographic Atlas of the World*, the Turkish edition of the *Encyclopedia Brittanica*, and *Nouveau Petit Larousse Illustre*. All of them have been declared "means of separatist propaganda" by Turkish authorities for containing articles or maps related to the history of the Armenians or the Kurds.

According to the United Press International in March 1986, Turkish censors have banned books ranging from Plato's *Republic* and the works of Maxim Gorky to Henry Miller's *Tropic of Capricorn*. The UPI quoted a librarian at the library in the American Embassy in Ankara as saying, "We have never had a problem here. But then, we simply don't order any book that deals with such sensitive subjects as the Armenians or Kurds."

Individual publishers have been sentenced to long terms in jail. Recep Marasli, 30, is serving sentences totaling 36 years in Diyarbakir Prison for publishing books about the Kurdish ethnic minority in Turkey and for alleged separatist activities. Amnesty International reports that he has taken part in several hunger strikes protesting torture and inhuman prison conditions, and is in poor health.

On March 19, 1987, *Cumhuriyet* reported that publisher Huseyin Kivanc had been released on bail of 300,000 Turkish lira. Kivanc had been in custody since May 13, 1986. He has been charged with propagating Communism via publication; the books he published, for which he is on trial, include two books by Lenin and three by Mao Tse-Tung. His trial started more than 10 years ago; the prosecutor originally asked for a sentence of 105 years-- 15 years for each of seven books--but has now reduced his request to 22 years and 6 months.

According to the PEN Turkish Writers in Prison Committee, 32 people have been sentenced to 750 years for writing or publishing; four have been released and investigations of 26 more are pending.

Academic Freedom

In its previous reports, Helsinki Watch described the tightening of controls and declining standards that have characterized Turkish universities and schools since the 1980 coup. There is no significant improvement in the state of academic freedom in Turkey today. If anything, this situation appears worse, as post-coup practices become more and more institutionalized and former academics despair of ever regaining their posts.

Incomplete lists compiled by a former professor at the Middle East Technical University (METU) in Ankara for the years 1980 to 1984, give the names of about 327 people who were fired and 861 who resigned out of a total of about 28,000 teaching positions in Turkish universities. At METU, which had a total faculty of 1300, a partial list contains the names of 17 people who were dismissed and 312 who resigned. Many of the academics who resigned did so for practical reasons: they had been told they would be fired under Martial Law 1402, and anyone fired under 1402 is thereafter barred not just from teaching but from any government job.

We were told that of the incomplete list of 327 academics who were fired from university teaching jobs, at least 74 had been dismissed under Martial Law 1402. After martial law was lifted, some 30 to 40 of these professors appealed their dismissals and sued for reinstatement. In 10 or 11 cases, the lower courts decided in favor of the academics; the universities appealed to the Higher Administrative Court, however, and final decisions have been reached in only four of the cases: Professors Baskin Oran, Mete Tuncay, Nurkut Inan and Yalcin Kucuk won their cases, but only one, Yalcin Kucuk, returned to teaching at Gazi University and then chose to retire. None has been reinstated on a permanent basis.

The Higher Education Council (YOK) controls the academic program and the staffing of the universities, which were autonomous before the coup. Academics who are still teaching at Istanbul, Bogazici and Ankara Universities gave us disturbing accounts of pressured, routinized, unfulfilling, underpaid jobs and seriously low morale of both students and faculty. One professor told us: "It's hard to keep your integrity, to keep calm. Those of us who have remained at the university feel isolated and lonely." The libraries are suffering from financial cutbacks resulting in fewer books and journals. A professor of electrical engineering told us that his personal library was larger than the library at Trabzon University, a technical university. At another university, faculty members pool money in order to subscribe to a few journals. Academics complain that little research is being carried out, and then only research that is congenial to the administration.

Several professors from Istanbul and Bogazici Universities told us that, although political repression is bad in those universities, it is much worse in the provincial universities, which are less privileged. The social sciences and humanities are suffering most severely. Ismail Besikci, a sociology professor recently released after serving ten years in prison for his sociological study of the Kurds and for a letter sent from prison criticizing the government, told us that scientific inquiry is not possible in Turkish universities today because of political constraints.

Academic skills are not enough for promotion: all teachers are subjected to government security checks, not once, but at every step in the hierarchy. We were frequently told by despondent academics, both within and outside the university system, that the quality of the universities has been destroyed to such an extent that, even if all the dismissed professors returned to the universities, it might take a generation to restore the high caliber of education that prevailed in Turkey before the coup.

Students, too, are suffering from discouragement and low morale. Each four-month semester is broken up into one and a half months of classes and two and a half months of exams--three mid-term exams and one or two final exams. Students feel that they are constantly studying for exams; teachers feel they are constantly reading and grading exams.

Since the 1980 coup the government has been concerned about student activities. The Constitution forbids students to join political parties; students are not permitted to establish national associations and they can be expelled for taking part in "ideological action." Recently the government proposed new legislation that would allow only one student association in each university, to which every student would automatically belong. There was an enormous outcry as a result: students protested, demonstrated and marched. At least one group of 63 students is on trial in Ankara before a state security court for such protest demonstrations; 31 of the defendants are in police custody. Apparently surprised by the severity of the protests, the Motherland Party has withdrawn the bill from consideration at this time by Parliament.

In a shady courtyard at Istanbul University we met with five students representing student associations from two faculties of Istanbul University and from Marmara University. All were upset about the government's proposed changes in student associations: the abolition of existing associations, a quorum that would require 50 percent of the student body to elect officers and make decisions, and the tight control to be exercised by the rectors of the universities. They told us that more than 500 students had been detained by the police in connection with demonstrations and protests about the student association regulation. Of these, 160 had been arrested and indicted. Those detained in Istanbul had spent an average of 50 days in custody; all had been released by the time of our visit, but the trials were continuing. The students are charged with violating the law on public meetings and demonstrations, for which the sentence could be from one and a half to three years. The protests took place in Ankara, Istanbul, Izmir, Adana, Eskisehir, Bolu and Edirne.

In the past year there have been many demonstrations by students on other university issues as well; many students have been detained as a result. According to *Info-Turk* (May 1987), State Security Courts have ordered the arrests of 52 students in Ankara, 31 in Istanbul and 300 in Izmir. Amnesty International has reported that over 600 students have been taken into custody and that detained students were tortured in Istanbul and Ankara. Amnesty, in a July 1987 newsletter, cites the case of Nilufer Aydur of Gazi University who says that she was tortured for ten days in police custody. On trial at Ankara State Security Court on May 26, 1987, she testified that she had been stripped naked, hosed down with ice-cold water and given electric shocks. When she still refused to sign a confession, a male student was brought to the room and forced to attack her sexually. She then signed a confession.

Both students and faculty told us of their concern about the rise of fundamentalism in the universities. (See *Religious Freedom.*) A teacher observed ironically that some universities had mosques but no libraries. Fifteen or 20 of the 28 universities in Turkey now have mosques. In 1987, during Ramadan, there were several incidents in which religious students harassed students who were not fasting, including a highly publicized case in Van, in eastern Turkey, in which religiously oriented students attacked non-fasting students in a cafeteria across from the University of Van. In the clash that followed, student Sirin Tekin died and seven other students were wounded, two seriously.

Religious Freedom

Turkey has been a secular state since it became a republic under Kemal Ataturk in 1923. Recent controversies concerning religion have taken two forms: on the one hand, a rise in Islamic fundamentalism and a concurrent fear on the part of many that the secular nature of the state is being compromised; on the other, protests by believers who assert that they are not permitted to practice their religion freely.

Article 24 of the Turkish Constitution supports both points of view. It states that "No one shall be compelled to worship, or to participate in religious ceremonies and rites ..."; at the same time, it also states that "Acts of worship, religious services, and ceremonies shall be conducted freely ..."

Former Prime Minister Bulent Ecevit told us that the "religious problem" has grown, citing enforced religious education in the schools as an example. He said that religious education became compulsory when the new Constitution was approved in 1982. Turkish children, 99 percent of whom are said to be Moslem, and in some cases even Christian children, are forced to attend religious classes that are predominantly Islamic in content. Children of Alevis, too, are forced to attend religious classes based almost exclusively on Sunni precepts, although the Alevi sect (comprising, according to Mr. Ecevit, as much as one third of the Turkish population) is a progressive branch of Shi'ism, with beliefs quite different from those of the Sunnis. Mr. Ecevit believes that recent acts of fanaticism in the universities, including the killing of a student in Van for not fasting during Ramadan, are the result of tolerance and support of fundamentalist groups by the government and the military.

Some academics believe that the Islamic movement is gaining strength and constitutes a danger to Turkish society because of its anti-democratic beliefs. They told us that the Kemalist state has always been concerned about two movements, communism and fundamentalism, but that after the 1980 coup, fundamentalism was for the first time permitted and supported. Nuri Colakoglu of *Milliyet* told us that people were worried that the Islamic fundamentalists in Turkey would develop into a force like the fundamentalists in Iran.

Several people described to us the Turkish-Islamic synthesis espoused by a rightist intellectual group that is trying to re-orient Turkey to Islam and away from the Western orientation established under Kemalism. The new ideology holds that, because Turkey is surrounded by enemies, Turkish culture, which is dictated by a 1000-year-old Turkish-Islamic synthesis, must be promoted. According to their critics, proponents of this ideology believe that democracy is a good political regime, but that anyone who rejects Turkish culture, as defined by the Turkish-Islamic synthesis group, should be banned from political activity and public life.

Various intellectuals told us of their fears: that the government would establish a fundamentalist state in the name of Ataturk; that Turkey would have

31

a new repressive government in the name of religion; that they would soon have to "live through another nasty experience, this time in an Islamic state."

The other side of the religious controversy is represented by Turks who believe the government does not allow them to practice their religion freely. We met, for example, with six young women, students at Istanbul University, who told us of their struggle to practice the Moslem religion as they saw fit by wearing headscarves to class. The women, ranging in age from 17 to 25, represented a new breed of fundamentalist women whose presence in Turkish society has become increasingly visible in Istanbul and Ankara: they wore rather somber headscarves that completely covered their hair, long coats that extended almost to the floor, and no make-up. Their spokeswoman, who asked that her name be withheld, was an intelligent and articulate 21-year-old student who spoke excellent English. She told us that women had been wearing headscarves to class without incident until February 1987, when the rectors of the universities got together and decided that headscarves should be banned from the classrooms. Women who wore the scarves to class were told to take them off or leave; some were suspended for from two weeks to two months. As a result, protests and hunger strikes erupted in many parts of the country. In Istanbul, students held a sitdown strike in front of the university from 10:00 until 7:00 every day for 21 days; the police did not make them disperse, but surrounded them. In Ankara, students engaged in a sit-in were scattered by the police; some who protested were taken into custody, beaten with truncheons and later released. Some students, both men and women, were arrested and detained for one day for sending a telegram to President Evren protesting the ban. The students' spokeswoman told us that students in Istanbul collected thousands of signatures protesting the headscarf ban; these were taken to Ankara and presented to Prime Minister Ozal.

The issue of headscarves apparently arose when President Evren said on television that students should dress in a modern fashion. YOK, the Higher Education Council, then suggested to the directors of the universities a regulation that women must dress in "contemporary garb." A fundamentalist journalist, showing us a stack of newspaper clippings about the headscarf issue that was about four inches thick, told us that more than 100 cases had been launched

32

against students who protested the headscarf ban, and that another 100 students had been thrown out of school. Wearing headscarves is a must for a Moslem, he believes. He pointed out that, although the number of women involved is small--about 5,000 --it is the tip of the iceberg: other women are under pressure by their families not to wear scarves in order not to jeopardize their education. As a result of the controversy, YOK now says that the decision is up to individual universities. Some universities have abandoned the regulation, but many have kept the regulation in force.

Because of their refusal to remove their headscarves, many young women were not allowed to take their final exams and have lost a full year in school. Some students have suffered additionally by being expelled from the university under a university rule that if you fail a course one year, you must pass it the next; students who were not able to take the final exam were therefore thrown out of school.

The controversy has caused emotional problems for many students. Some have been forced to give up their principles and take off the scarves. Others are in deep trouble with parents who do not want their daughters to jeopardize their futures by refusing to attend class. "My future is not as important as my belief," one of the young women told us.

Many non-religious Turks are also troubled by the headscarf controversy. They respect the right to religious freedom, but worry about the growth of religious fanaticism in Turkey. Some blame it on the military's encouragement of religious education in the schools. Some theorize that the increased involvement in religion in the universities was the result of the repression of other outlets for student activities. A few questioned the official response to the headscarf controversy, pointing out that the fundamentalist student protesters were treated much more leniently than, for example, leftist student activists. The *Turkish Daily News,* September 29, 1987, reported that a State Security Court in Konya had acquitted nineteen students charged in connection with demonstrations against the headscarf ban; sixteen were women.

We met in June with some fundamentalist journalists who described their concerns about religious repression. They asked us not to use their names, pointing out that to express their religious beliefs in political action violates Article 163 of the penal code, which prohibits any attempt to advocate a non-secular state and stipulates a sentence of six years in prison or 15 years each if two people take action together. One of the journalists told us that even carrying religious thoughts in his head is worrisome and that he lives in constant fear.

Some of their complaints are that mosques, which are supposed to be social and cultural centers, are locked between prayer services; that mosques are run by civil servants; and that the Department of Religious Affairs sends out scripts for preachers to use at Friday services, rather than allowing them to prepare their own. They believe that Moslems should be permitted two hours free from work to go to the mosque on Fridays; that Moslems should be permitted to wear beards (one bearded journalist showed us his identity card with a photograph of him cleanshaven; he could not have gotten an identity card showing him with a beard); and that Moslem women should be permitted to have women doctors attend them at childbirth in the state hospitals. They charged that the one fortieth of a Moslem's income which, by religious law, he is supposed to donate to Islam, is taken by the government which gives it to state foundations that have no religious purpose.

The journalists believed that Turkey is not the secular state that it claims to be because it intervenes in religion, rather than allowing its citizens to practice religion as they see fit. "The main problem," said one of the journalists, "is that the government wants us to put our hearts on coat hangers when we go into an official building, and put our brains on hangers when we go into a mosque."

The government continues to bring prosecutions in religious cases:

- The *Turkish Daily News* reported on July 10, 1987, that Hasan Damar was on trial in Ankara at the State Security Court on charges of defaming Turkey abroad and propagating the establishment of a Sharia regime in Turkey.
- According to *Ankara Anatolia*, July 14, 1987, authorities have launched an investigation against the imam of a mosque in Bursa for preaching that watching television is sinful.

34

Freedom of Movement

On April 13, 1987, *Cumhuriyet* reported that since 1980 300,000 Turkish citizens have been denied passports, and therefore the freedom to travel abroad. The newspaper said that 20,000 are restricted because they owe back taxes. Anyone against whom a criminal case is pending is not allowed to travel abroad. The rest are denied passports at the discretion of the Minister of the Interior.

Prime Minister Ozal told *Der Spiegel* in March 1987 that he gives direct exit permits on a case-by-case basis upon recommendation of the Ministry of the Interior. Abdullah Basturk, leader of the trade union DISK, was permitted to go abroad during the DISK trial on such a basis, as was Alparslan Turkes, of the right wing National Movement Party. Other artists and intellectuals have also received special permission for individual trips, but many have not. Orhan Apaydin, former head of the Istanbul Bar Association who was a defendant in the Turkish Peace Association case, sought permission to go abroad for medical treatment; permission was ultimately granted, but Mr. Apaydin died on that very day.

Because officials were unwilling to meet with us during our June 1987 fact-finding mission to Turkey, we were unable to discuss passport denials with the government. On April 14, 1987, however, *Milliyet* reported that the Ministry of the Interior claimed that 26,800 Turkish citizens were at that time prohibited from leaving the country; of those 6,800 were forbidden to leave because "their presence abroad would be deemed incompatible with general security conditions." The rest were prohibited for non-payment of taxes. *Milliyet* claimed that the number of people denied passports was actually 370,337 as of April 1, 1987.

Cumhuriyet of April 13, 1987, quoted Article 22 of the Passport Law which lists categories of people who are denied passports:

> Those who are under general security surveillance and those who are banned from traveling abroad by court order, those who cannot prove that they can provide for themselves abroad, those whom the Minister of Interior has deemed undesirable to leave the country for general security reasons, those who owe taxes.

35

Those who are on trial for, or have been convicted of, crimes such as crimes against the state, encouraging prostitution, smuggling arms and ammunition, embezzlement, extortion, fraud, certain crimes related to the Labor Law, crimes that mandate heavy sentences, crimes with an ideological or political intent.

Those who are defendants will not be issued passports or travel documents until they have been acquitted, or the charges dismissed; those sentenced must complete the sentence before a passport will be issued.

Those determined undesirable for staying abroad will not have their passports renewed.

Cumhuriyet also reported that many prominent lawyers, artists and writers continue to be denied passports, including writers Bekir Yildiz and Atilla Ozkirimli, singer Selda Bagcan, musician Timur Selcuk, directors Zeki Okten and Serif Goren, actors Tarik Akan and Genco Erkal, lawyers Gulcin Cayligil and Turgut Kazan. Relatives of "undesirables" are also often denied passports, including the daughter of Mehmet Ali Aybar, the president of the defunct TIP (Turkish Workers Party), and, in 1984, Gursel Apaydin, the wife of Orhan Apaydin. Turgut Kazan, a lawyer, told us that "no one knows how many people have been denied passports--it could be 300,000, it could be 600,000." He said that the Ministry of the Interior keeps the figures at the Data Center, but that no one is permitted to see them.

Murat Belge, a leading intellectual and editor of *Yeni Gundem*, has been without a passport since 1981, allegedly because of a negative report by the MIT (national intelligence agency). He told us he was planning to reapply. Another writer told us that he was able to get a passport because he "knew someone who knew someone" at the passport office.

Ali Taygun, a stage director who is a graduate of the Yale School of Drama and was a defendant in the Turkish Peace Association trial, has been invited to stage a play for the American Repertory Theater, but has been denied a passport. Ruhi Su, a prominent singer, was denied permission to travel abroad for treatment before he died of cancer a year ago.

Deprivation of Citizenship

Article 66 of the Turkish Constitution provides that: "No Turk shall be deprived of citizenship, unless he commits an act incompatible with loyalty to the motherland." Despite this constitutional protection, according to *Cumhuriyet*, April 6, 1987, 13,788 Turks living abroad have been stripped of their citizenship since the 1980 coup; of these, 8,945 have lost their citizenship in the past four years.

In February 1981 Law No. 403, the Turkish Citizenship Law, was amended to state:

> Those who happen to be abroad, and engage in activities detrimental to the internal or external security of the Turkish state, or its economic interests, may, upon being summoned to return to the country and subsequent non-compliance, be made to lose their citizenship. *(Ozurluge*, September 1986.)

Writing in *Cumhuriyet* on July 30, 1987, lawyer Turgut Kazan said:

> Turkey's practice of divesting individuals of their citizenship is chiefly linked with military considerations. According to Article 25/C of Law 403, citizens who live abroad and who do not respond when called up for military service are stripped of their citizenship. ... However, we are well aware that our people fail to respond to the call-up not because they are afraid of military service, but because they dread losing their jobs.

Among those who have been deprived of their nationality, according to *Info-Turk*, July and August, 1986, are trade union officials Yucel Top, Gultekin Gazioglu, Mehmet Karaca, Aydin Yesilyurt, Murat Tokmak, Halit Erdem, Bahtiyar Erkul, Semsi Ercan, Metin Denizmen, Kemal Daysal, Zeki Adsiz, Yasar Arikan, Muslim Sahin, Yucel Cubukcu, Sahabettin Buz, Sait Kozacioglu; journalists Dogan Ozguden, Inci Tugsavul, Umran Baran, Askin Baran, Kamil Taylan, Latife Fegan; writers Mahmut Baksi, Huseyin Erdem, Mehmet Emin

Bozarslan; artists Yilmaz Guney, Melike Demirag, Sanar Yurdatapan, Cem Karaca, Fuat Saka, Sahturna Dumplupinar, Hadi Ormanlar; lawyers Beria Onger, Huseyin Yildirim, Serafettin Kaya; the Chairwoman of the Workers' Party of Turkey (TIP), Behice Boran; and the Chairman of the Socialist Party of Turkish Kurdistan (TKSP), Kemal Burkay. According to Turkish sources, Cem Karaca was allowed to return to Turkey during the summer of 1987.

According to Mustafa Ekmekci, writing in *Cumhuriyet*, Dec. 2, 1986, about eighty men of letters have lost their citizenship since 1980; included are poet Nihat Behram, writer Demir Ozlu, and journalist Yagmur Atsiz.

In March 1987 the Democratic Left Party, according to the *Turkish Daily News,* March 24, 1987, submitted to Parliament a proposed law that would amend Law No. 403; the preamble of the proposed amendment said that most of the Turks who had been deprived of citizenship were in fact "individuals who truly believe in democracy, the Republic, and wholeheartedly respect the integrity of Turkey, but oppose the official view and ideology of the [present] government." The preamble went on to say that there were also "Turks who went abroad for the purpose of finding employment. Because they were illegal aliens in those countries, they had to apply for asylum to find work. The way to save these Turks [is] not to strip them of citizenship, but to pardon them."

Political Freedom

Political parties in Turkey continue to be free to criticize the government. Parliamentarians raise embarrassing questions on the floor of Parliament. The Turkish press often prints comments by opposition politicians that are highly critical of Prime Minister Ozal and his ministers. All of these are encouraging signs of an active, energetic democratic system.

In another encouraging development, the Turkish electorate voted by a narrow margin on September 6, 1987 to rescind Provisional Article 4 of the Constitution, which had banned former politicians from taking part in politics. The ban had affected about 100 people, including former prime ministers Suleyman Demirel and Bulent Ecevit.

Despite the ban, Mr. Demirel and Mr. Ecevit had spoken publicly for many months before the referendum. During our June visit, Mr. Ecevit told us that about 130 legal cases are pending against him for speeches he has made in violation of the ban, and that about 45 are pending against Mr. Demirel. Mr. Ecevit has been acquitted on several of the charges, but, on December 29, 1986, he was convicted on one charge and sentenced to 11 months and 20 days in prison; the case is now on appeal. If Mr. Ecevit's sentence is upheld, he will, as a result of a provision in Article 76 of the Constitution, be forbidden from ever again running for Parliament. According to the *Turkish Daily News* of September 8, 1987, the court cases are continuing and could still result in denying Mr. Ecevit the right to run for election. Meanwhile, Prime Minister Ozal has called for general elections in November 1987.

Mr. Ecevit pointed out other limits on political freedom imposed by Article 76; for example, a person who has been banned from public service may not be elected to Parliament. Under Martial Law 1402, the commanders were allowed to expel anyone from public service without stating a reason or applying to a court for permission, and that person would then be barred from serving in Parliament. A person who served a year in prison for a street brawl or other minor offense at a young age would not be able to run for Parliament later. Article 83 prohibits a labor union executive or an executive of a public professional organization from serving in Parliament. And Article 68 prohibits students and university faculty members from belonging to political parties.

Although voting is mandatory in Turkey, Provisional Article 16 of the Constitution provides that voters who did not vote in the 1982 referendum on the Constitution would not be permitted to vote for five years. According to Mr. Ecevit, this means that about two million voters who, as a protest, did not vote on the Constitution are still forbidden to vote.

The government remains firmly in control of Turkish Radio and Television (TRT). This means that Prime Minister Turgut Ozal can use television for political purposes, while very little time is given to the statements or actions of other political parties. On July 29, 1987, the *Turkish Daily News* reported that the TRT Executive Board had turned down a petition by Suleyman Demirel for television coverage; the TRT decided that news about banned political leaders should not be televised. On July 1, 1987, the Ankara public prosecutor started an investigation against Correct Way Party Chairman

Husamettin Cindoruk for slandering Prime Minister Ozal; Ozal had complained that Cindoruk had called him a traitor.

During the campaign for lifting the political bans, the opposition parties alleged harassment by the government. The *Turkish Daily News*, July 24 and 25, 1987, reported that during a campaign tour of the Social Democratic Peoples Party, (SHP) in late July 1987, Fikri Saglar, the SHP Secretary General, was beaten up by policemen in uniform when he tried to prevent a plainclothesman from taking photographs of people who had come to listen to SHP Chairman Erdal Inonu.

Freedom of Assembly

Perhaps the most striking change for the good since the last Helsinki Watch mission to Turkey is in the areas of free assembly and association. Public meetings, demonstrations and protest marches are now being held on a scale that would have been unthinkable a few years ago. As with other newly acquired freedoms in Turkey, there are no legislative guarantees for those who choose to exercise their rights; in some cases participants in public activities have been detained, beaten, tried and sentenced, but in others the police have taken no adverse steps at all.

Within 48 hours of our arrival in Istanbul, we attended a public meeting organized by the Association of Families of Detainees and Convicts, at which a panel of speakers discussed prison hunger strikes, torture of detainees and other abuses that their relatives in prison are enduring. An audience of some 300 individuals included young and old, well-dressed and poorly-dressed; many wore red carnations, and some women carried small bouquets. Some of the older women wore headscarves. Many people cried openly during the accounts. The audience also participated by singing prison songs and reciting prison poetry. We were told that some members of the group who had hung posters announcing the meeting had been detained by the police before the meeting began, but were released after the association protested. Once the meeting began, there was no interference, although at one point sounds of a walkie-talkie were heard at the back of the hall. When we left the hall, a man in civilian clothes was photographing the participants. There was also a police van parked outside, and the photographer seemed to be on comfortable terms with the policemen inside.

Students at Istanbul University held a rally to protest the Higher Education Council regulations on June 2lst. As a part of their application for a permit, they submitted a list of the slogans that they were planning to use at the rally. Several were banned, including "Down with Fascism," "Down with Imperialism," and "Workers, Youth and Peasants Unite." The police told them that political slogans would not be permitted -- only slogans that had to do specifically with student problems. We were told that two students were interrogated for 20 minutes by police before being released.

During our visit to Turkey, we were urged to meet with several new organizations formed to represent specific interest groups. The fact that such "fringe" groups are seeking an independent existence is a positive indication of a movement toward pluralism in Turkey.

We met, for example, with representatives of a newly formed homosexual and transsexual rights group. They told us that 100 people had demonstrated in Istanbul's Taksim Square in April to protest police brutality against transsexuals and transvestites; they were joined in the demonstration by groups representing feminists, greens, atheists and anti-militarists.

In Ankara we saw a small group of environmentalists preparing to hold a demonstration in Guven Park in Kizilay, in the center of the city. Guven Park is an old park with trees and benches and a children's garden; the demonstrators were protesting the municipality's plans to cut down the trees to make a car park.

On the other hand, the Human Rights Association reported in September 1987 that a group of 190 relatives of prison inmates traveling by bus to Ankara to demonstrate for better prison conditions were stopped by police at the entrance to the city. In the scuffle that followed, police beat marchers and reporters. One marcher, Didar Sensoy, the diabetic sister of an inmate, collapsed an hour later and died. Another marcher, Leman Firtina, alleged that Sensoy collapsed because of beating and stress. In addition, three reporters were beaten and their cameras were either broken or confiscated. Sixty demonstrators were detained for eight hours.

41

Freedom of Association

Freedom of association is also an area that has witnessed considerable improvement. Many associations have sprung up and are now operating, some with permission from the government, some without.

To our eyes, the most encouraging of such developments is the establishment of a Human Rights Association (HRA). The group is based in Ankara with a branch in Istanbul, incipient branches in Adana and Izmir, and plans for branches in other cities in the future. All new associations must submit their statutes to the Ministry of Interior; the HRA did so three times before being approved in December 1986. It was initially denied approval on various grounds: that its aims were not clearly spelled out, that the Association might attempt to usurp areas of competence belonging to the state, or that it might engage in politics. The association was obliged to amend its statutes to satisfy the authorities.

The aim of the HRA is to defend human rights in Turkey. It has about 560 members throughout the country, although it has not conducted a membership campaign, preferring to remain relatively small. Anyone can join the group. The 98 people who founded the group on July 7, 1986, included lawyers, writers, doctors, journalists, relatives of prisoners, architects, and engineers. Nevzat Helvaci, the president of the association, told us that the group does not concern itself with the political outlook of its members. Although no well-known rightist has joined as yet, Mr. Helvaci says that all are welcome.

In Ankara we met with Mr. Helvaci, Akin Birdal, the association's general secretary, and board members Erbil Tusalp and Mahmut Tali Ongoren. The HRA seems well established: its rented office consists of two rooms and a reception area; there is a paid secretary and a part-time janitor. Helvaci, a lawyer, spends a good deal of time on organization matters--as much as full time, when necessary. Neither he nor the other officers are paid. The association is supported by dues and contributions from individuals as well as income from fund-raising events; members pay annual dues of 6,000 Turkish lira (less than $10).

The HRA's ambitious program includes producing reports and holding press conferences and panel discussions. It has issued a report on 170 people who have died in detention since the 1980 coup, and a report on prison conditions. Mr. Helvaci said that they receive six or seven phone calls a day asking for help with problems, not all of which are human rights problems. On the day that we visited their offices, ten people had come to the office with human rights problems; one was a woman whose husband had been taken to police headquarters three days earlier; when he was brought home it was obvious that he had been beaten or tortured.

The Istanbul branch, which has 200 members, has sponsored three or four panel discussions: on the proposed penal code, on women's rights and on torture. It has also helped individuals with human rights problems--victims of torture, for example.

The HRA is not allowed to have a formal relationship with a foreign organization, but maintains informal contacts with other groups and exchanges information.

A number of other associations have also started functioning; one is the Association of Families of Convicts and Detainees, discussed under *Freedom of Assembly.* Another is the homosexual rights group described in the same section. Feminist groups have formed in Ankara and Istanbul; each has held demonstrations protesting the beating of women. The Ankara demonstration took place on a rainy Mother's Day in the center of the city; 15 women carried small placards asking that women not be beaten, and passed out flowers. Police observed the demonstration but made no efforts to stop it; one young woman told us she thought the police had not taken them seriously. She also told us that people on the street seemed interested in their program, and that their strongest opposition comes from Turkish Marxists who believe that feminism is a diversion from concentration on the class struggle. A much larger demonstration for women's rights took place in Istanbul in June when about 3,000 people marched. An Association of Ex-Faculty Members was started in Ankara in November 1986. It is made up of former university professors who were dismissed from positions by martial law commanders under Martial Law 1402. *Cumhuriyet* reported on January 14, 1987, that the Minister of Interior had rejected the group's application; we were told by a faculty member in Ankara that the group is currently being investigated, but has not been banned.

The Turkish Writers' Association, which was shut down after the 1980 coup, and whose executives were on trial for four years and finally acquitted, has re-opened; its first general congress was held in March, 1987. The Turkish-Greek Friendship and Peace Association, formed in May 1987, is awaiting approval; meanwhile a goodwill delegation of five members acting on their own behalf visited Greece in October as the guests of a similar Greek association.

As is often the case with positive developments in Turkey, this is not, unfortunately, the whole picture. Two other associations have been denied permission to operate, and furthermore some of their founding members have been investigated and are being prosecuted. The first organization was started by a group of doctors--Physicians for the Prevention of Nuclear War. This group started up in April 1987 and was banned two weeks later by the governor of Ankara. In a letter dated April 30, 1987, Assistant Governor Yahya Gur stated that the association's articles had been examined by the Ministry of the Interior, and went on to say:

> ... random explanations made by the members and officers of an association who have absolutely no responsibility in such a delicate and total war as nuclear war may cause public panic; Furthermore ... the aims and subjects of activity adopted by your association coincide with those of the Turkish Atomic Energy Institute and the Civil Defense Directorate of the Ministry of Interior Affairs, and hence might produce an ambiguity in function and authority.

The public prosecutor subsequently opened a case against 49 founders of the organization. The doctors have said that the trial against them is outrageous and, according to the *Turkish Daily News* of June 9, 1987, have so far refused to testify about their activities.

Bulent Akarcali, deputy chairman of the Motherland Party, stated at a luncheon at the U.S. Ambassador's residence that another doctors' group that had advocated the abolition of the death penalty had acted improperly; it should have dealt with medical problems like hospital conditions, instead of involving itself in "political" issues. The doctors' group in question was put on trial for seven months and acquitted in September 1986. We were later told that the doctors' group had in fact taken positions on specifically medical issues in addition to its stand on the abolition of the death penalty.

A second association that is in trouble is the Association for the Purification of the Turkish Language. Turker Alkan, a former professor of political science at Ankara University who is now an advisor to the Social Democratic People's Party (SHP), told us that the group was closed down by the governor of Ankara because he believed that the government should carry out such activities. Another former professor told us that the government believed that the association was a leftist conspiracy to destroy Turkish culture and align Turkey with the USSR; he did not agree that the association was a political group, but saw it as a group that wanted to go back to the original purposes of the Ataturk Institute, set up by a bequest in Ataturk's will--to rid the Turkish language of Arabic and Persian words.

The Turkish Peace Association

In *Freedom and Fear* we reported that:

The most notorious political case in Turkey is that of the leaders of the Turkish Peace Association (TPA), some of the most prominent people in Turkey, including the former president of the Istanbul Bar Association, the former head of the Turkish Medical Association, the former general secretary of the Turkish Writers Union, the wife of the former mayor of Istanbul, a former diplomat and ambassador, former members of parliament, and a number of prominent writers, journalists and intellectuals. Of the original 26 TPA leaders brought to trial, six have been imprisoned for more than three years; six were released from prison in 1984, six were just released on February 17, 1986, and the others have managed to leave Turkey or are in hiding. A retrial of the case is continuing.

The Turkish Peace Association, a legal organization before the coup, was founded in 1977 by the Istanbul Bar Association to promote nuclear disarmament, compliance with the Helsinki accords and the peaceful settlement of international disputes. Many of its leaders were active supporters of former prime minister Ecevit. The group considered itself a "Helsinki group," with its focus on the security provisions of the Helsinki accords, rather than on human rights compliance.

At the end of April 1987, a verdict was reached in the latest TPA trial. The TPA was found to have been:

> an illegal society with the purpose of establishing the domination of a social class over other social classes or exterminating a certain social class or overthrowing any of the established basic economic or social orders of the country.

The association was banned and its property confiscated. In addition, twelve defendants were convicted and given prison sentences. The case is now on appeal.

Two members of the executive committee, Mahmut Dikerdem, the president, and Reha Isvan, the wife of a former mayor of Istanbul, were convicted and sentenced to four years and two months. Eight others, Dr. Erdal Atabek, Prof. Dr. Metin Ozek, Aykut Goker, Orhan Taylan, Huseyin Bas, Nedim Tarhan, Erol Saracoglu and Ataman Tangor, were convicted of:

> founding within the country an organization which has its roots abroad, without the permission of the government; organizing activities outside of the stated aims of the association; engaging in international activities in violation of the Law of Associations

and sentenced to one year and six months. Niyazi Dalyanci and Nurettin Yilmaz were sentenced to six months for engaging in international activities in violation of the Law of Associations.

The court "separated" the files of four other defendants, Ali Taygun, Gundogan Gorsey, Sefik Asan and Ataol Behramoglu, who had been convicted of identical charges in a case against the Communist Party of Turkey. The final decision in their cases was delayed until the completion of the appeal in the Communist Party case.

Charges were dropped against Orhan Apaydin and Ismail Hakki Oztorun, who died during the trials; charges against nineteen other defendants were dropped because of a statute of limitations; the case against Sadun Aren was dismissed; the cases against Turgan Arinir and Ayfer Coskun were postponed in their absence, and twenty-seven others were acquitted.

Since all of the convicted TPA members had already spent considerable time in prison, most of them will not have to serve any more time if the sentences are upheld, but two--Ataman Tangor and Erol Saracoglu--would have to serve an additional seven months and eleven days. The others have spent more time in prison than the sentences they were given, ranging from one month and fifteen days to two and a half years. Among those acquitted, nine had served from nine months and 22 days to over three years in prison.

Several of the TPA defendants told us that they thought that international interest in their case from groups such as Helsinki Watch and Amnesty International had shortened their sentences. Gencay Saylan, a former political science professor who was acquitted after having spent three years and 25 days in detention, told us in Ankara that all the convicted TPA members are working, although some do not have "proper jobs." Because of their convictions, all state jobs are closed to them, which makes it very difficult to find work; the state is a major employer in Turkey.

Professor Saylan is now a journalist; when we asked him how he felt about losing three years of his life, he shrugged and said:

It's gone--it's a very common thing; mine was not an individualistic case. After a while, going to prison seems like a natural thing--part of life in Turkey.

He said that although the experience has left him angry, and uneasy in the presence of military people, it has not made him more radical or changed his political outlook substantially. He went on to say:

The experience was more difficult for my family, especially for my daughter, who was in high school. My wife works for the U.N., which was lucky for the family. If she had been working for the government or for a Turkish company, she very well might have been fired--lots of wives were.

Prof. Saylan told us that he had kept up his friendship with other members of the TPA. The solidarity of the group was evident, too, at a dinner we attended in Istanbul with other former members of the TPA.

47

Trade Unions

Restrictions on trade union rights appear to have changed very little since our previous mission in December 1985. The problems faced by trade unions in organizing workers and in carrying on traditional union activities are rooted in restrictive Constitutional provisions and labor laws that sharply curtail trade union actions.

Ruchan Isik, the International Labor Organization representative in Turkey, told us in his office in the UN building in Ankara that Turkey's trade union laws do not comply with ILO standards, particularly with regard to freedom of association and the right to bargain collectively. The ILO has strongly recommended to Turkey the revision of Laws No. 2821, the Trade Union Law, and 2822, the Collective Bargaining, Strike and Lock-out Law. Although the ILO has had discussions with the Ministry of Labor and has been told that the government is concerned about these issues and would like to make changes, no changes have been made thus far.

According to *Cumhuriyet*, June 9-14, 1987, Turkey was criticized sharply during the 73rd ILO conference in Geneva in June 1987 by European trade unionists for its labor policies and for having taken no action on a letter of intent sent in 1986 to the ILO, in which the government had promised to change the labor laws.

The December 1986 Bulletin of the Department of International Affairs of the AFL-CIO lists the Turkish labor code's "objectionable features" as:

About 500,000 teachers and 1.3 million other Government workers are prohibited from joining or organizing a union;

A unionist must work in an office or plant for ten years before he or she can be an officer in a union representing that work site;

Before being able to enter into a collective bargaining contract for workers in a plant or office, a union must not only have a membership of over 50 percent at that work site, but must have signed up at least 10 percent of all workers in its whole work branch (e.g., 10 percent of all steel workers).

48

The right to strike and picket is restricted in numerous ways. For example, no more than two persons are allowed to picket, and the only words permitted on a picket sign are "This work place is on strike." The law gives the Government so many options to postpone or cancel a strike that in practice this right can seldom be used legally;

Union collection of dues for strike and solidarity funds is forbidden.

In June 1987 the *Anatolia News Agency* reported that the ILO's Applications Committee had handed a "final warning to the Turkish government to improve its anti-democratic labor and trade laws"; the committee's report said it was "deeply concerned" about trade union rights and freedoms in Turkey.

In September 1987 the AFL-CIO recommended to the United States Trade Representative that Turkey be denied the benefits of the Generalized System of Preferences because of its "cavalier attitude toward internationally recognized worker rights." The AFL-CIO also recommended in June 1987 that Turkey be denied "most favored nation status" unless trade rights improve in the near future.

While we were in Turkey, Abdullah Basturk, the president of the now-defunct Confederation of Revolutionary Trade Unions (DISK), was in Geneva at a meeting of the European Confederation of Trade Unions. The *Turkish Daily News* of June 13 and 14, 1987, reported Mr. Basturk's comments that the relevant articles of Turkey's Constitution and union laws were so full of anti-democratic legislation that it would be impossible to compare them to European trade union practices; "Turkey is still way behind the standards of European democracy."

We met in June with Emin Kul, general secretary of Turkey's largest union, Turk-Is. Mr. Kul was serving as acting president while the union's President, Sevket Yilmaz, was out of the country attending an ILO conference. He told us that Turk-Is had continually made "great efforts" to change the labor laws. "From time to time the government has asked us to be patient and told us that changes would indeed be made. But they haven't." As a result, Mr. Kul said, Turk-Is's relations with the government are tense.

49

Discussing the worst aspects of the present labor laws, Mr. Kul described the same problems described by the AFL-CIO, cited earlier. He added that trade unions have difficulties in ruling themselves, because their income and expenditures are controlled by the government. Every year two officers from the Ministry of Labor and the Ministry of Finance go over their figures and all financial documents to decide whether their expenditures conform to the purposes of the trade union. Trade unions cannot set their own membership fees, or extra fees, nor can they spend money on or lend money to affiliates. And, of course, trade unions are not allowed to take part in politics; no union official can express a political view.

Three officials of Yol-Is, the Road, Construction and Building Workers Union, which has 140,000 members, described the labor laws as "a huge agglomeration of restrictions" and discussed the problems listed earlier. They told us that under present conditions it was almost impossible for a union to conduct a successful strike. Some unions, for example those in energy, banking and mining, are forbidden to strike at all. Others are permitted, but if no agreement is reached, the dispute can be sent to the Supreme Arbitration Council (SAC), which, they believe, has awarded unfairly low wage increases to workers. They said that because the laws and policies are not conducive to strikes, there have been few strikes, representing a relatively small percentage of the work force.

An official of Otomobil-Is, an independent union with a membership of about 60,000 automobile workers, told us that no union leaders are in prison at present. "Many leaders have left the country because of repressive labor conditions, however," he said, "and are working as trade unionists in Europe, or as workers."

In March, Turk-Is attempted to stage a protest march in Ankara. Police stopped the march, and, according to the international edition of the *Turkish Daily News* of March 31-April 6, 1987, the prosecutor of the State Security Court questioned members of the executive committee about the march for five hours before releasing them. The *Turkish Daily News* quoted a number of members of Parliament as saying that the protest action failed beause

50

of defects in the country's laws. One said, "The country's laws even prevent unionists from marching on the streets."

The DISK Trial

On December 23, 1986, the trial of the Confederation of Revolutionary Trade Unions (DISK) ended in a decision which abolished the union and sentenced 264 DISK officials to prison terms of up to 15 years. The military tribunal in Istanbul also disbanded 28 of DISK's 31 member unions. The trial had begun on December 25, 1981; it involved 1,477 trade unionists who were charged under article 141 of the Penal Code with trying to "establish the supremacy of one social class over another."

According to a report in *The Financial Times* of December 27, 1986, "... no convincing evidence ... was produced by the prosecution." *The Guardian* called the number of convictions "unacceptably high." DISK Chairman Abdullah Basturk and General Secretary Fehmi Isiklar were among those who were sentenced to 10 years' imprisonment; 54 others received 5 to 10 years, while 1,169 were acquitted. Ceytin Uygur, a member of the DISK executive council and the leader of Yeralti Maden-Is (Underground Metal Union) was sentenced to fifteen years and eight months. Some unionists estimate that another 2,000 trade union leaders have fled Turkey to avoid prosecution. During the trial, many of the defendants said they had been tortured. The case is now on appeal.

Several trade unionists told us that the decision has had a major impact on them; they believe that if DISK could be disbanded by the courts, any other union, including the largest, Turk-Is, could be shut down at any time.

51

III. TORTURE

For some years now, Turkish authorities have claimed that torture is no longer used in Turkey, except for an occasional case of police brutality. But Helsinki Watch, in all of its previous reports on Turkey, has found torture to be widespread and common. Unfortunately, this remains the case: on our recent visit we were forced to conclude that torture is still practiced in Turkey on a large scale.

Virtually everyone with whom we discussed torture--with the exception of a Foreign Ministry official and the deputy chairman of the Motherland Party--told us that torture continues in Turkey; many believe that it is a deliberate policy of the government. Many cases of recent torture have been documented by the Turkish press, by international human rights organizations and by Helsinki Watch during our fact-finding mission in June. Among the people we interviewed were two who had been tortured brutally at the infamous Gayrettepe police station just a few weeks before our visit; we photographed Gayrettepe from a distance and had pointed out to us the floor on which the tortures take place.

Because we were denied visits with the Prime Minister, the Ministers of Justice and Interior, the Chief of Police, and members of their respective staffs, we were unable to discuss with them the use of torture in Turkey or to document the government's efforts to discourage or minimize torture and to punish torturers. Many of the government officials with whom we sought to meet, however, have discussed such matters with the press.

During our visit, Chief of Police Saffet Arikan Beduk was interviewed on torture in *Cumhuriyet* on June 16, 1987. Referring to Turkish police who have been convicted for using torture, he acknowledged that "small incidents have occurred," but called it "a pity that some of our friends have been punished" since they "worked with good will" and merely made "some mistakes." Mr. Beduk flatly denied that torture exists in Turkey; he said that there is no

53

deliberate or systematic torture, and that people who accuse the police of torturing them are lying.

Prime Minister Turgut Ozal also denies the existence of torture in Turkey. In a special advertising section printed in *The Wall Street Journal* on May 26, 1987, Mr. Ozal said, "The Europeans talk about torture. There is no torture today in our prisons. None at all." Asked by *Der Spiegel* on March 16, 1987, "Is there no torture any more under your government?", Mr. Ozal replied, "No, all the allegations have their sources in the previous period." In response to a question by *Le Monde* on December 13, 1986, Mr. Ozal said that if a case of torture or brutality was alleged, it was not only reported in the press, but charges were filed and proceedings brought by an independent attorney. "The fact is that emphasis is placed on events dating back to the military regime," he went on, "which are portrayed as topical cases. There have been no such cases recently. In my opinion there is no human rights problem in Turkey. Allow me to add that if a representative of the law and order forces makes a mistake it is his fault, not the system's."

Umur Apaydin, head of the Council of Europe Department in the Foreign Ministry, one of the few government officials with whom we were allowed to meet, told us in Ankara in June 1987 that "claims of torture are the fashion in Turkey." He asserted that just about everyone who goes through police custody later claims to have been tortured, and that many interrogators are resigning as a result. "Isolated cases exist," he told us, "but they can't be stopped despite manifold instructions of high-level government officials." He told us that instructions on preventing torture were sent to all police stations from time to time; when we asked to see a copy, he said he would find out whether he could release one, but we have not heard anything further from Mr. Apaydin on the matter. "You can't change the approach of an individual police officer," he said. "It's a question of culture and requires a long process of education. Torture is not a problem that's peculiar to Turkey; it's a problem for all police forces everywhere."

In our interview with Bulent Akarcali, deputy chairman of the Motherland Party, he also made the point that police abuses exist in every society, including the United States and Europe. He believes that the police in Turkey are punished for such abuses, and that accusations of torture are made by people on the far left who are trying to discredit the government and destabilize the country. He believes that economic and social destabilization will lead to martial law and military intervention. "Don't forget," he said, "we came from a period of almost civil war--anarchy in which thousands were killed. You can't allow people to discredit the civil police system; if they are discredited, you will need martial law again."

Mr. Akarcali emphasized the need for well-educated, well-trained civil policemen with maturity and self-confidence. The government has fired thousands of policemen, he told us, and opened a police academy at the university level which has cost billions in Turkish lira. The government has worked closely with the United States and Germany in training the police, he continued. High-ranking police have been sent to the United States to inspect police work there, and American specialists have come to Turkey for educational training--electronic techniques of interrogation, video-tape interrogation, etc.

Nevzat Helvaci, the HRA president, announced in June 1987 that 240,000 Turkish citizens had been arrested in the seven years since the 1980 coup and that the great majority of those detainees had been subjected to torture and maltreatment.

On June 11, 1987, the *Turkish Daily News* reported that Minister of Justice Oltan Sungurlu denied allegations of systematic torture in Turkish prisons and said that investigations were conducted frequently when complaints of torture were made. In January 1987, Mr. Sungurlu had told the *Turkish Daily News* that the government was "staunchly against the practice and incidence of torture in Turkish prisons and is determined to bring all those responsible before the courts."

Tercuman reported on December 22, 1986, that Justice Minister Sungurlu disclosed that 13 people had been tortured to death in Turkey since the 1980 coup. But others have reported that many more than 13 people have died as a result of torture. It was reported in *Nokta*, May 11, 1986, that Fikri Saglar, the deputy chairman of the SHP, had announced that 78 people had died from torture since September 1980. The Turkish Human Rights Association in a 20-page report dated February 12, 1987, said that of 149 people who had died in detention since 1980, 97 had died from torture and 14 from lack of treatment after torture; 24 were said to have committed suicide, 10 died from hunger strikes against prison conditions, and four died in clashes with security forces. When we met with the Human Rights Association in Ankara in June, they gave us a supplementary list of 20 more people who had died in detention (the full list of 169 names is attached as Appendix 2), and told us that these lists are not complete. According to the HRA, some of the torture deaths were witnessed by as many as 14 people. During a July news conference, the HRA announced that the number of deaths in detention had risen to 170.

Nevzat Helvaci, president of the Human Rights Association, told the press in February 1987 that many of the deaths were said to have taken place between 1980 and 1983. The HRA believes that torture is still widespread. "Those who go inside still complain of torture," he said. "It looks as if there has been no change in the methods. They still use electric torture, make people stand naked in cold water and apply *falaka* (beating the soles of the feet). If torture is not as prevalent as before, the reason is that the number of people taken into custody now is less." The report claims that some of the alleged suicides were in fact deaths as a result of torture.

The Human Rights Association demanded that "an urgent inquiry be held into those cases where none has been held, and that those responsible be brought to justice." In fact, nothing has been done. The government has never denied that 170 people have died in detention, although some authorities have accused the HRA of using the list for political purposes.

The Human Rights Association has posed a number of questions to Turkish authorities on torture: Why do torture investigations stall for many years? What was done about the officials named in former torturer Sedat Caner's confession? Is pressure put on doctors to issue false reports indicating a person was not tortured? What legal basis is there for the promotion and rewarding of officials convicted of or under investigation for torture? Who is behind torture; why can't torturers be found even when torture has been proven?

Fikri Saglar, general secretary of the SHP, told us in June that Parliament is looking into torture in response to the HRA's report. He said that he has personal information on torture as well, and has asked the SHP to draw up plans for a report on torture. He also told us that there has been no official response to a list that he presented in Parliament in 1987 of 253 political prisoners who have either died during interrogation or disappeared after detention since 1980. (See Appendix 3.)

The HRA's release of the list of deaths in detention has been criticized by some; Baki Tug, a military prosecutor during the military intervention of 1971-73 and currently an official of the Correct Way Party (DYP), termed the list as "exaggerated and with suspicious motives." According to *Cumhuriyet*, February 15, 1987, Mr. Tug said that he was against arbitrary torture, but "How are our police to make captured bandits and robbers talk? ... Torture is a crime against humanity, but one cannot remain with hands tied vis-a-vis murderers and robbers who are enemies of the state. ... The purpose of torture claims is to weaken the prestige of the state and encourage criminals."

International human rights organizations have concluded that torture is still going on in Turkey. Amnesty International, in a report issued on June 15, 1986, declared:

> Throughout 1986 and to the present date Amnesty International has continued to receive allegations of torture and deaths caused by torture and believes that any person detained for suspected political offences is in danger of being tortured. Most allegations of torture relate to the initial detention period which under Turkish martial law amounts to 30 days and under regular law to 15 days in cases involving three or more suspects. But even these detention periods, during which suspects are denied access to lawyers or close relatives, are often extended. ... Amnesty International is concerned that Turkish law allows such lengthy periods of *incommunicado* detention. Internationally recognized standards require that detainees be brought promptly before a judge or other judicial officer (Article 9(3) of International Covenant on Civil and Political Rights)...

In October 1986 the Vienna-based International Helsinki Federation for Human Rights (IHF) sent a fact-finding mission to Turkey to look into torture and political prisoners; the members of the mission were Erik Siesby, Chairman of the Danish Helsinki Committee and Professor of Law at the University of Copenhagen; Jerry Hayes, a British Parliamentarian; and Gerald Nagler, executive director of the IHF in Vienna. An IHF report based on the mission, issued in March 1987, concluded that: "In our opinion it is beyond reasonable doubt that torture practices continue and that the instances of torture cannot be reduced to isolated instances of police brutality."

The IHF report included figures given by the Minister of Justice on March 14, 1986, on torturers brought to trial. The figures are different from the ones cited above, which were released by Minister Sungurlu in December 1986. The March statement indicated that 3,077 allegations of torture and ill treatment had been investigated, that 546 persons had been sentenced to imprisonment of from two months to life, that 2,418 persons had been acquitted of charges against them, and that legal proceedings were continuing in 1,722 cases. Because the Minister of Justice was not allowed to meet with us, we were unable to determine the reasons for these discrepancies.

There is a rehabilitation center in Denmark for victims of torture. *Nokta* reported on December 12, 1986, that Dr. Ugur Celasun had visited the center and that 28 Turks had been treated there. Dr. Celasun said that not everyone was accepted at the center: first, refugee status has to be conferred by the Danish government; then Amnesty International has to confirm that the person had actually been tortured.

Teoman Evren, President of the Union of Turkish Bar Associations, told us in June: "Not enough action has been taken on torture. Statesmen have not taken definitive actions to end torture, and courts have not followed up torture allegations with sufficient care. The attitude of officials who do not pursue torturers encourages more torture. Statesmen make statements that give heart to torturers, for example, saying that torture takes place all over the world--in Sweden, in the United States." He quoted the Minister of the Interior as saying that "anyone who has a mark on his body says he was tortured." He told us that President Evren had said some time back that those who in previous days tortured and killed one another do not have the right to complain now of torture by others.

Mr. Evren gave us a number of recommendations calculated to eliminate torture:

> Detainees should be able to see their families at any time;
> detainees should be able to see their attorneys at any time;
> detainees should be examined by doctors of their choice;
> the period of detention should be shortened;
> convicts should not be taken from prison for questioning;
> the state should make a definite change in its attitude toward torture;
> there should be an easier process for investigating and prosecuting people accused of torture;
> the penalties for torture should be increased.

The Union of Turkish Bar Associations is limited in what it can do to bring about these changes; bar associations are forbidden by law to engage in political activity.

Torture is very hard to prove, according to Mr. Evren. Except in cases of death or lasting injury, the traces of torture usually disappear after 15 days. "In the old days," he said, "suspects had to appear the very next day before a judge. Now suspects can't even see their lawyers for 15 days or, in some cases, longer. In general, torture occurs during those periods."

Former Prime Minister Bulent Ecevit told us that he believed torture could be largely ended by allowing people who are detained to talk to their lawyers at any time; as noted earlier, his party plans to re-submit a bill to that effect in the Parliament. He believes that torture and arbitrary killings are continuing and points out that reports in the press of individual cases of torture are not denied by the government.

Suleyman Demirel, another former prime minister, told us that torture is continuing, that 175 or 180 people have died from torture, and that torture is the policy of the current government.

Erdal Inonu, head of the Social Democratic People's Party (SHP), told us that most torture no longer takes place in prisons, but in detention centers. He, too, favors immediate access to defense counsel for detainees and believes that unannounced inspections of police stations would reveal electric shock and other equipment used regularly for torture. The electric shock equipment and other instruments of torture would then have to be taken away.

Turgut Kazan, an attorney with many years' experience in the practice of criminal law, told us that the majority of his clients have been tortured. "I know it's very difficult to believe what I say," he told us. "Some things I have difficulty believing myself." As an example, he told us about a case in which the police, in an effort to make his client confess, brought in his wife and child and gave electric shock to the five-year-old child. Although both his client and his wife told him about it, Mr. Kazan told them he didn't believe them. The wife said, "Why should I lie to you?" Eventually Mr. Kazan came to believe that they were telling the truth. The incident took place in August 1986.

Nejat Yazicioglu, a member of the Istanbul Medical Association, condemned the part that doctors play in the torture of prisoners. Speaking as part of a panel discussion organized by the Association of Families of Detainees and Convicts, he declared:

> In Metris Prison physicians were always present at torture; their function is to determine how much a victim can take. These physicians should not be acquitted of their acts--I speak as a physician. When the medical association found out, we said we would take steps to press charges against any doctor who took part in torture. We are still on trial for that statement ... How does someone turn into a torturer? He becomes part of a system that uses torture as a form of government. Anyone who witnesses torture and does nothing becomes a partner in crime--torturers are civil servants paid by the government... If a physician is present and does nothing, he is also a party to the crime. Torture is not aimed so much at the individual--once he's been through it he's not afraid anymore--but at the total society which fears it.

Ismail Besikci, a sociologist who was released on May 25, 1987, after serving three separate sentences totaling over ten years in prison for his writings on the Kurds and for a letter criticizing the government, told us from his prison experiences that torture is a state policy in Turkey, and that if you talk about it, you are considered an enemy.

Professor Mumtaz Soysal told us that there is less discussion of torture in the press now, after the furor that arose over the detailed disclosures in February 1986 by former policeman Sedat Caner who admits to having tortured over 200 people and described the specific techniques that he and special torture units used in torture. The public's interest has diminished, according to Prof. Soysal. "People are used to torture; it's almost in bad taste to keep writing about it," he said. He believes that there may be somewhat less torture now, and that this may be linked to Turkey's application for full membership in the European Community.

Turkey has not signed the United Nations convention against torture. Amnesty International continues to urge the government to do so, most recently in June of this year.

Recent Cases of Torture

In Istanbul in June, we met with Nurhan (not her real name), a slender, nervous 26-year-old woman, mother of a two-year-old child, who was brutally tortured, together with three other women, during police detention in April 1987. The four women were accused of distributing subversive literature which they claim never to have seen. Nurhan was taken into custody after being named by one of the other women, whom she knew only slightly. The following is our summary of what she told us.

> At the Gayrettepe police station the women were beaten, stripped, given electric shock, and subjected to intense water pressure and *falaka*. The husband and son of one woman were brought to headquarters; the police threatened to torture them and told the husband they would rape his wife if he did not tell them what they wanted to know. The husband then signed a statement saying whatever the police wanted him to say. The husband, wife and child were then released.

> Although Nurhan was blindfolded throughout the torture, the leather blindfold slipped out of place from time to time when she was being beaten, and she saw that she was in a large room with a rug on the floor, rubber tires and a big closet. The police tore her stockings at the toes and tied electric cables to her smallest toe and to the little finger on her right hand. Then

61

they sent electric currents through her body, stopping to ask her again and again where she lived. They then repeated the shocks on the left side and doused her with cold water to intensify the pain. On the first day this went on from 3:00 P.M. until 9:00 P.M. "It's not the electricity that hurts," she told us, "it's the convulsions, and hitting yourself during them."

As the days went on, Nurhan was beaten with fists and with something that felt like iron. She was stripped to her slip and bra and given electric shocks. She was beaten on the face, arms and legs, sometimes sitting, sometimes lying on the floor. Currents were sent through all her fingers and toes and her navel. Later she had wounds where the cables had been fastened--her hands swelled and were still red. In between shocks she was interrogated, sometimes by a woman, sometimes by men.

From time to time, in what amounted to four days of torture, the police brought in the other two women, each of whom had been tortured even more severely than Nurhan. One woman had had a nightstick shoved in her rectum and was in such bad shape she couldn't sit down. One had been beaten so badly she had a hard time talking. Each at various times had been suspended from a cross: a thick piece of wood wrapped in cloth that was attached by chains to the ceiling. Their arms were tied to the crosspiece with a piece of cloth; one woman was suspended in that fashion for four hours. The women told Nurhan that after they were on the cross the electric current felt good--it seemed to repair the damage from the cross.

One evening the police told Nurhan that they would come to get her at night to give her "a small operation." She was terrified and didn't sleep all night, but no one came. The next day she began admitting things and ultimately signed a statement prepared by the police. The day before they were to appear before a judge, the women were taken from their cells for exercise, examined for wounds and other problems, and allowed to wash their hair. The following day, in the State Security Court, they renounced their written statements, telling the judge that the statements were extorted by torture. Nurhan

62

was released from custody, but the case against the women is continuing. As a result, she has lost her job and has been unable to get a new one. Her husband has gone into hiding because the police are looking for him, too. She told us that she was very nervous, had lost a lot of weight, and had not been able to eat or sleep for some time after her release. When we asked her if she had asked to see a lawyer while she was in Gayrettepe, she laughed and said: "They would have told me I'd been seeing too many American movies."

The facts of Nurhan's detention were confirmed, not only by her lawyer but by a 17-year-old girl who had been detained on different charges in Gayrettepe police station at the same time as Nurhan. This young woman was also beaten and tortured in the police station; she asked that we withhold both her name and the facts of her case. She described, however, her encounter with one of the women who was a defendant in Nurhan's case. Through a peephole in her cell door, she could see her being taken in and out of her cell:

> She looked awful. She told me that the woman in the cell next to hers could not walk, she had been beaten so badly on the soles of her feet. I saw the others being roughed up, pushed and dragged away.

A young man who was badly tortured in Gayrettepe in 1980 and 1981 told us in June that two of his friends had been arrested within the past six months for taking part in a protest march and severely tortured. He described the experience for us:

> First you're blindfolded; then you start feeling blows--you don't know where they're coming from. It's a terrible feeling of isolation, of loneliness. You hear the cries of other people being tortured--they make sure you hear them. There's no discrimination between men and women--the inquisition begins by stripping you. Then you are given electric shocks on your lips, ears, nose, fingertips and genitals. You are given *falaka*. Then you are suspended on the wall; in ten minutes you lose consciousness. You are given water torture and are beaten with sacks full of sand, to leave no marks. When they

get really crazy they insert truncheons in your anus. Women are threatened with rape, and sometimes raped.

His friends told him that they had each been tortured for 15 days, using the same techniques that had been used on him; then they were sent to the public prosecutor, who found there was not enough evidence to hold them, and they were released.

Many people, in Istanbul and Ankara as well as in southeast Turkey, told us that torture was most severe and widespread in the Kurdish areas of Turkey. This was borne out by interviews we conducted with Kurdish refugees in Canada in April 1987; some of their stories appear in this report in the section on *The Kurdish Minority*.

Both former Prime Minister Bulent Ecevit and Kadir Nardin, a member of Parliament from Diyarbakir, described the case of Adnan Tuysuz, an agricultural worker from the village of Ceylanpinar in Urfa in southeastern Turkey, who died while in custody in February. He quoted Tuysuz's wife, who said he was taken to the gendarmerie, and that she and their four children were later taken to the gendarmerie as well. She said that the soldiers tortured her husband in her presence and later released her. The police subsequently told her that her husband "had been shot while trying to escape during the reenactment of the crime at the scene" in a mine field near the Akrepli region on February 17, 1987. His wife believes that he was tortured to death.

Cumhuriyet reported on March 31, 1987, that Tuysuz had been detained for questioning about an arms cache found near the Syrian border on February 9. His body has not been found. Vecihi Atakli, an SHP Member of Parliament from Sanliurfa, has petitioned Minister of the Interior Yildirim Akbulut about Tuysuz's death, asking why Tuysuz was taken to a mine field for a "reenactment" at 3:00 A.M., why the body had not been recovered, and why the battalion commander had not been relieved of duty during the investigation.

The Turkish press continues to report cases in which people have died in detention, allegedly as a result of torture:

- Esma Bayram alleged in February that her husband, Zulfikar Bayram, was beaten to death at a police station in Diyarbakir (in the southeast) where he was taken for questioning about his son,

64

who is wanted by the police. She said that seven other family members were beaten with rifle butts at the same time. The Diyarbakir prosecutor said that Bayram had been beaten to death. Bayram's son, 22, said: "The commander, Mustafa Hasturk, hit my father first on the head with a rifle butt. Shortly after that my father started vomiting. After the beating at home was done, the soldiers took us out; some remained. My father's vomiting increased and he was unable to walk. When he muttered, 'I am dying,' Hasturk said, 'You are Greek, I am going to kill all of you.' The soldiers dragged my father and took him to the station."

Responding to questions on the Bayram case, Minister of the Interior Akbulut said: "Torture is a crime, but torturers exist, even if in small numbers. The cases are all investigated and it is wrong to comment publicly on a case under investigation. There are widespread allegations of torture in Turkey. This is a political or ideological approach ... The ulterior motive in such allegations is to prevent the security forces from pursuing criminals. It is not correct to blame all the institutions for a crime committed by isolated individual officials." *Cumhuriyet*, February 23 and 24, 1987.

- Orhan Erdagli started a brawl at a bar in Beyagac in Denizli in February. He was taken to the gendarmerie station, where he swore at Private Cevdet Erog; Erog shot and killed him. Erog was arrested. *Cumhuriyet*, February 24, 1987.
- Mehmet Kalkan was apprehended for an ordinary crime and imprisoned in Diyarbakir in 1983. He escaped soon afterwards, was picked up in March 1987 and detained at Diyarbakir Police Headquarters. His brother charged that he was killed there during torture. Police said that Kalkan hanged himself with a rope. Two members of Parliament from Diyarbakir investigated. M.P. Seyhmus Bahceci reported, "It is not possible that Kalkan committed suicide. Where could he have found the rope? Furthermore, any suspect taken there is searched down to his buttons." *Cumhuriyet*, June 21, 1987.
- On August 16, 1986, in Ankara, torture was revealed in an autopsy of the body of Yuksel Tokdogan who had been pronounced dead by the police during interrogation. It was noted that the victim had been paralyzed a week before his death. *Info-Turk*, July/August 1986.

- Mumin Yasar Serdar, 18, died after being beaten at a police station to which he had been summoned to get his security clearance for his future residence at the Middle East Technical University dormitory. He died of leukemia from which he was already suffering at the time of the beating. Sergeant Erhan Yuksel, who beat him, was suspended and taken to court. *Cumhuriyet*, November 5, 1986.

There have also been many recent reports of torture which did not end in death:

- On December 22, 1986, Yilmaz Onay, a dramatist, stage director and translator, was taken into custody while rehearsing a play; his son, Gokhan Gercek, was detained the same night and released the next day. Gercek said on his release that he had heard his father being tortured under high pressure water. Onay, 50, was taken to the Ankara State Security Court on December 26th and released. No charges were filed against him.

Onay said after his release that he was pushed into a room and told to "start confessing," because his captors "knew everything. I said I could not think of any crime I may have committed. Then they just beat me up. They punched and slapped my face, then told me to talk before things got worse. But I had nothing to tell them." Onay, who remained blindfolded throughout his ordeal, said he could hear other prisoners screaming in pain. "They ordered me to strip naked. Suddenly a jet of cold water hit me from behind. ... When I could no longer scream the jet was turned off. I was ordered to jump up and down. I guess it was to stimulate my circulation. Then the jet came on again, this time from the front."

He said he has no idea how long the water torture lasted. When it ended, he was questioned again. "I realized they had nothing on me but wanted me to confess to something. I could not. Then they hung me on a rack by my wrists, still naked and with my feet dangling." When he still refused to confess, Onay said, "they put an electric wire on my feet, then my knees, then my thighs and finally on my genitals. I guess I was screaming like hell."

Onay was never told why he had been detained. He suspects it was because police found his name and address in a notebook confiscated from a friend of his son's who had attended a meeting to discuss forming a socialist party. *Chicago Tribune*, February 26, 1987; *Cumhuriyet*, December 25, 1986, through January 2, 1987.

- Teacher Ahmet Yilan was detained in December 1986 and later arrested for being a member of an illegal organization. A medical report dated January 5, 1987, attested to his having been tortured. Sihali Yalciner, the chief editor of "Demokrat Karaman," was also detained and tortured. Yalciner held a press conference after his release at SHP headquarters in Konya and said they were tortured for six days. "They put us through cold water. They beat us, especially at night. For six days I was made to wait in the cell standing up. I could only buy milk and cookies on the day I was released. An official gave me an anti-acid for my sick stomach on the last day." *Cumhuriyet*, January 8, 1987.

- In Pulumur, in Tunceli province, on September 3, 1986, a young woman named Necla Yuce was arrested by police and given a gynecological examination to find out whether she had recently had sexual relations with her husband, who is sought as an alleged PKK member. *Info-Turk*, September 1986.

- Amnesty International reported in *Continuing Violations of Human Rights in Turkey*, June 15, 1987, that Mehmet Aytunc Altay was detained for 49 days in February and March, 1987, and charged with membership in the Turkish Communist Party. He said that during his detention he was tortured by means of hanging, electric shocks, cold water baths, beatings and squeezing of his testicles.

It is beyond the scope of this report to list all of the allegations of torture that have appeared in the Turkish press in recent months. The above is just a small sampling. Sometimes a policeman or security force officer is charged, more often not.

Punishment of Torturers

During Helsinki Watch's December 1985 mission to Turkey, we found that the authorities had taken some steps to punish torturers. We reported figures on prosecutions, convictions, dismissals and sentences provided by the Parliamentary Committee for the Inspection of Prisons and Detention Houses in September 1985, by Prime Minister Turgut Ozal in the same month, and by a

Hurriyet columnist in January 1986. We also noted that the figures were inconsistent.

The March 1987 International Helsinki Federation report referred to earlier in this section included figures given by the Minister of Justice on March 14, 1986, on torturers brought to trial; the statement indicated that 3,077 allegations of torture and ill treatment had been investigated, that 546 persons had been sentenced to imprisonment of from two months to life, that 2,418 persons had been acquitted of charges against them, and that legal proceedings were continuing in 1,722 cases. According to *Tercuman*, December 22, 1986, Minister of Justice Sungurlu reported that in 1986 legal actions were brought against 1,459 people accused of violating Articles 243, 244 and 245 of the penal code's chapter on the maltreatment of individuals. He also said that sentences had been passed on 100 of the accused during 1986.

In January *Nokta* reported that Minister of the Interior Yildirim Akbulut had disclosed that since September 12, 1980, 758 policemen had been subjected to legal proceedings for torture and mistreatment of detainees or prisoners. He also said that 684 officers were on trial, 74 had been convicted, 294 acquitted, and 260 cases were continuing. These figures, inconsistent with the numbers supplied by the Minister of Justice, add to the confusion.

Because neither the Minister of Justice nor the Minister of the Interior agreed to meet with us, we were unable to ask them or any members of their staffs about these differences. As a result, we cannot say for sure how many people have been prosecuted and sentenced for torturing detainees or convicted prisoners. What we can say is what we said in our last report: that relatively few torturers have been convicted in relation to the number of cases brought, and that the number of cases that have been brought bears little relationship to the actual number of torture victims in Turkey.

Asked about the punishment of torturers, Teoman Evren, president of the Union of Turkish Bar Associations, told us in June that the Minister of Justice says that torturers are being punished, and that if he says so, it must be true. "But there are certainly many more torturers than the number that have been punished," he added. He pointed out that it is very difficult to complain about torture and very difficult to prove it.

Many Turks with whom we discussed the matter agreed with Mr. Evren's assessment of the difficulty in bringing charges against a torturer. First, victims are routinely blindfolded, so that they may never see the faces of the officers who mistreat them. Second, they are not allowed to see lawyers or family members until they are formally arrested; by that time (15 or 30 days later) most marks of torture have cleared up. Third, if they are sent to a doctor for a medical report, the doctor is chosen by the military, and his allegiance is to the military and not to the victim. All of these factors obviously make it extremely difficult, if not impossible, to prove torture to the satisfaction of a court. But there is another major deterrent: many victims are afraid to bring charges, for fear they will be detained again, and again mistreated by the same torturers.

A lawyer with whom we talked in Mardin, a town in the southeast that is 30 kilometers from the Syrian border, told us in June that many of his clients have been tortured by police or members of the gendarmerie--the security forces. He has opened cases against the police, and has one case continuing at present. He told us about a case that had taken place eight months earlier in Nusaybin, a village of Mardin; four policemen beat people and gave them electric shocks in order to force the victims to give them money. The beatings took place both inside the police station and outside the station. When the chief of police found out about it, he suspended the four officers for three months; they are now back at work. Charges have been brought against them by the public prosecutor. The victims themselves were afraid to sue the police for damages for fear the police would beat them again.

The Mardin lawyer told us it is very difficult to bring a case for money damages against the police. "Although the law permits such suits," he said, "they are rarely successful, and if they are, the damages awarded by the courts are extremely low because the value of human life is low. The amount of the award is up to the judge; there are no legal limits. In practice, if the damage to the victim is substantial, he or she will be paid the equivalent of the minimum wage for the lost earnings. If the damage was not substantial, a victim will be awarded between 5,000 and 10,000 Turkish lira [about 6 to 10 dollars], an amount clearly not conducive to encouraging people to bring suits."

A young man in Istanbul who had spent more than five years in prison for belonging to a left-wing political group told us in June: "Although Turkish authorities say that torture is illegal, that torturers will be punished, and that a victim can get redress in the courts, even money damages, in actuality those things don't happen." He knew of no one who had sued for torture; his friends don't report torture to the authorities or to the press. "The authorities take no action and the newspapers don't regard torture as news--torture is habitual in Turkey." As an example of the lack of seriousness with which authorities regard charges of torture, he told us about a police officer who was the chief of a torture team of four persons and was charged with killing someone by torture; although the case is still pending, the officer has been appointed chief of police in a large section of Istanbul.

The Turkish press continues to report cases of police officers being tried, and sometimes convicted, for torture:

- A police chief sergeant, two sergeants, one aide and one policeman were on trial in October 1986 for the death in custody of Behcet Dinlerer, a Dev-Yol defendant, in December 1980. *Cumhuriyet,* October 16, 1986.
- Mustafa Hayrullahoglu was taken into custody for belonging to TKP on November 14, 1984, by a police team in Istanbul which included police sergeant Umit Bavbek. Hayrullahoglu was brought dead to the Haydarpasa military hospital on November 16, 1984. A military court sentenced three policemen, including Bavbek, to ten years and eight months each on April 1, 1986. The case was appealed. Meanwhile, Bavbek was promoted. *Cumhuriyet,* November 28, 1986.
- A police commissioner and six policemen were tried in October 1986 for the death of Enver Sahan, who was taken into custody for arms smuggling in Gaziantep. Sahan had become severely ill during his interrogation, and was taken to the state hospital; he was then to be transferred to Ankara, but died on route on November 12, 1983. *Cumhuriyet,* October 30, 1986.
- Three policemen were tried in November 1986 for torturing Bektas Ayyildiz, owner of the Ayyildiz Publishing House. Ayyildiz said he was taken to the police station by officers Lutfi Denizli, Naci Ugur and Bekir Bostanci, after they found some pornographic publications while searching his premises. The publisher was tor-

70

tured for five days, including being given electric shocks after being drenched with water. *Ozgurluge*, January 1987.

- Remzi Karaoglu was detained in Burgazada after he helped extinguish a forest fire and later went to the police to warn them of a flare-up of the fire. The police were annoyed that he was involved in matters that did not concern him, beat him and took him to the police station, where he was given electric shocks and threatened. The chief of police later charged him with insulting the police; he was acquitted in January 1987. Karaoglu then charged the police with torture. Officers Hasan Oguzhan and Dursun Takar are on trial; the prosecutor is asking 3 months to 3 years. *Nokta*, February 8, 1987

- Superintendent Ahmet Akyurek was found guilty by a military court in Erzurum of causing the death by torture of Metin Aksoy, an alleged member of an illegal left-wing organization. Akyurek was sentenced to three months in jail. *Turkish Daily News*, March 3-9, 1987.

- Police chief Naci Isik and his deputy Halil Cinar were found guilty of causing the death by torture of Bekir Trasli, suspected of carrying a revolver, in Antakya. Each was sentenced to three and a half years and fined around $3,000. *Ankara Anatolia*, April 1, 1987.

- In March 1987 a trial was begun of five policemen charged with the torture death of Hasan Hakki Erdogan, an alleged member of TIKKO. Witness Hamdi Eroglu, who was in custody at the time, testified that Erdogan was "put on the hanger" nude and given electricity to the small fingers of his right hand, his foot and sexual organ for 45 minutes, then made to eat salt and drink water. Then he was placed nude in a tire and given electric shocks; after that he was given *falaka* and beaten for an hour. He bled from the mouth and had large wounds from the hanging. The policemen said that the wounds found by the coroner happened while they struggled with Erdogan when he tried to escape. *Nokta*, March 15, 1987.

- A prison director, Sabri Nakipoglu, was detained for trial by a court in Sivas for abusing his authority by approving torture and forcing political prisoners to commit suicide. Nakipoglu served as director between 1980 and 1986. Twenty-nine guards have been detained on similar charges and will be tried. *Turkish Daily News*, June 12, 1987

71

In its June 15, 1987, report, *Continuing Violations of Human Rights in Turkey*, Amnesty International wrote:

> The Turkish authorities have admitted the existence of torture but have repeatedly claimed that these were isolated incidents and that each incident would be investigated thoroughly and those found guilty of torture would be punished. In fact, Amnesty International is informed of many cases where torture allegations have not led to any investigations at all or where charges have been dropped at an early stage. Amnesty International has noted the fact that in some cases alleged torturers have been given awards and promoted by the authorities while investigations and trials against them were continuing.

IV. THE PRISONS

Political Prisoners

It is extremely difficult to determine how many political prisoners are now being held in prisons and detention centers in Turkey. In the March 1986 Helsinki Watch report, *Freedom and Fear: Human Rights in Turkey*, we combined figures for civilian and military prisons and estimated that:

> ... there were 12,349 convicted political prisoners in Turkey as of September 1985, and another 5,606 political suspects in detention.

That made a total of 17,954 political prisoners in prison or in detention centers.

"Official" figures printed in *Cumhuriyet* on January 1, 1986, indicated that there were 15,569 political prisoners as of November 1, 1985.

On February 4, 1987, Fikri Saglar of the SHP was quoted in *Cumhuriyet*: "At the present time ... nearly 10,000 people are in prison for crimes of thought." Amnesty International also estimates that there are 10,000 political prisoners at present.

The Chicago *Tribune*, February 26, 1987, reported:

> International human rights organizations estimate that the number of political prisoners in Turkish jails has dropped by half during the last two years, to an estimated 6,000 to 8,000 people.

According to Mumtaz Soysal, a professor of constitutional law at Ankara University:

> People now think that about 5,000 to 6,000 political prisoners are still in prison--that does not include people in detention centers. Fewer political prisoners are in detention centers because most of the large trials have ended; there are probably fewer than 2,000 detainees at present.

Yeni Gundem on May 10, 1987, listed seven on-going mass political trials; the seven involve 4,156 defendants, of whom 573 are in detention. *Info-Turk* in June 1987 reported that trials of hundreds of Kurdish militants should be added to that list.

Nevzat Helvaci, President of the Human Rights Association, estimates the number of political prisoners at 18,000--12,000 convicts and 6,000 detainees--but said this is not a "healthy figure." ANAP deputy chairman Bulent Akarcali told us that the number of political prisoners had been greatly reduced because of releases pursuant to the Reduction in Sentences Act; he had no accurate figures to give us, however.

Because the Ministers of Justice and Interior would not agree to meet with us, we were not able to discuss these contradictory figures with responsible government officials.

As for the total number of prisoners in custody--common prisoners as well as political prisoners--Justice Minister Sungurlu was quoted in *Tercuman*, December 25, 1987, to the effect that, although the number of prisoners and detainees had fallen to 40,000 after the Reduction in Sentences Act went into effect, it had risen again to 52,711--31,396 convicted prisoners and 21,315 detainees. He did not say how many of the 52,711 had been convicted of crimes of thought.

In June, Umar Apaydin of the Foreign Ministry gave us figures of 50,000 for the civilian prison population: 31,000 convicted prisoners and 19,000 detainees. He said there was a "negligible" number of detainees in military detention centers--about 1,100; if convicted, detainees in military detention centers are transferred to civilian prisons. He told us that the government did not distinguish between political and common crimes and could therefore not tell us how many people were in prison for crimes of thought.

Amnesty

Talk about the possibility of a general amnesty for prisoners, which seemed to have died down after the passage of the Reduction in Sentences Act in March 1986, is now reviving. According to the *Turkish Daily News* of September 21, 1987, the Human Rights Association started a campaign on September 19 to grant a general amnesty for "tens of thousands of people imprisoned after the 1980 coup ... in the name of peace, liberty and democracy."

Government officials are still on record as opposing an amnesty; Prime Minister Ozal told *Der Spiegel* in March 1986:

> Since the existence of the Republic our parliament has used the amnesty instrument about 20 times. I am strictly against using it now, because it would tempt people to assume they can do what they please because of a later amnesty. Instead, we will change our punitive action in such a way that prisoners will only have to serve 40 percent of their time if they show good conduct.

Cumhuriyet, October 23, 1986, reported one of Justice Minister Sungurlu's first statements to the press:

> I am against general amnesty, because the conditions for amnesty have not come about yet.

On September 3, 1987, the *Turkish Daily News* reported that Minister Sungurlu said that the Justice Ministry had done "no work" on the subject of a general amnesty, that the Motherland Party did not favor it, and that they would call for a general amnesty when "the time is ripe for it in Turkey."

Prison Conditions

In *Freedom and Fear* we described prison conditions that can best be characterized as inhumane: physical and emotional abuse of prisoners, dreadful physical conditions, non-existent or inadequate medical and dental care, inadequate food, little provision for exercise or fresh air, little contact with the outside world by letter or visit, reprisals against prisoners who revealed prison conditions to outsiders, chaining prisoners together on trips to courts or hospitals, hunger strikes to protest prison conditions. In 1987, we found little significant change. The one exception, to be discussed in detail later on, is that beatings and torture of convicted prisoners in prisons have lessened considerably since 1984.

In March 1987 a parliamentary delegation made up of Fikri Saglar, Ibrahim Tasdemir and Cuneyt Canver of the SHP, Alpaslan Pehlivanli of the

ANAP and Hasan Altay of the DSP, inspected the maximum security and semi-open prisons in Ankara. They were accompanied by prosecutor Ali Cagatay, prison director Nurettin Komurel and the general director of prisons and detention centers.

In a press conference following the visits, reported in *Cumhuriyet*, March 5 and 6, 1987, Fikri Saglar described inadequate and unhealthy conditions, insufficient food (daily food allowance is 325TL--less than 50 cents; one loaf of bread costs ll7 TL), and referred to the maximum security prison as a "house of pain," rather than a rehabilitation center. Ibrahim Tasdemir described problems in receiving mail, denial of radios and cassettes, and facilities that were "embarrassing." Cuneyt Canver said, "The prison is not conducive to living in by human beings." When we met with Fikri Saglar in Ankara, we asked him whether the parliamentarians' commission had visited other prisons. He said the commission had stopped functioning; the government had not liked its report on the prisons in Ankara.

In a report on the same visit, *2000'e Dogru*, March 8-14, 1987, reprinted a petition presented by prisoners to the parliamentarian commission which asked for:

1. Improvement of food, given that "the health of the people in prisons rapidly deteriorates, and the results of torture surface after one or two years;"

2. Freedom to communicate; correspondence takes l5 to 30 days to be delivered;

3. Freedom to wear clothes that prisoners would provide, instead of uniforms "which are directed at breaking the individual's morale;"

4. Single band radios and tape recorders to learn foreign languages;

5. Permission for out-of-town families to visit on other days than prescribed visiting days;

6. Permission for families to stay with patients who are hospitalized;

7. Elimination of the practice of keeping people in chains while waiting their turn at court, and of chaining two people together while using the toilet;

8. An increase in visits from once every two weeks to once a week;

9. Permission for prisoners to receive flowers.

The prisoners also complained about the practice of taking convicted prisoners out of prison and back to police stations to be interrogated further.

Nokta, on March 8, 1987, published a memoir of Faik Inal, a retired lieutenant general and former director of Hasdal Military Prison. Recounting his early days as Hasdal director right after the September 1980 coup, he said:

"The prisoners would be sent in groups of 30 or 40. I would shout my orders to them ... 'you'll do so and so, otherwise I'll break your heads,' etc. The newcomers are usually very tense since they are fresh out of the hands of the police. They think they are going to be beaten. If they are coming from another prison they expect a 'welcome beating.' For this reason, the tension starts from the very first day. We didn't have 'welcome beatings,' but beatings in other types of situations; for example, the thing that angered me most was prisoners shouting slogans. If they would not stop, I would enter the wards with clubs. The privates would stop them by beating them with clubs.... I personally beat prisoners with a club in the wards.

"Searches of wards are routine; they don't last more than half an hour. But to pressure the inmates one can extend the search for hours. Long searches and banning outdoor exercise are means of psychological pressure. If the purpose is to intimidate the prisoner, one can do the search every two days, morning and night. All these are up to the prison director.

"There were four toilets for 300 prisoners. The toilets are outside the ward. A man has to wait all day to go to the toilet.

77

Sometimes the ward door is not opened to punish the prisoners; that is when they would start beating on the door. Because some part of the man is about to explode. The single greatest complaint is about the toilet. Baths, visits, lawyers' visits were all problems. The law of the state says 'the prisoner is to sit at a table with his lawyer.' What we did was to parade the bayonets in front of the lawyer who would be behind barbed wire. Once I had a lawyer physically thrown out...

"I would take [political prisoners] to common criminals' wards, because common criminals don't have problems with the prison administration--a common criminal knows how to behave. He stays at attention and says, 'yes, my commander.' I would show such wards to the auditing commander, who would ask me how I managed to do it. I would answer that it was due to education. Educating all prisoners to become like this was the goal.

"Interrogation is not the job of the prison director, but one has to make do... The legal counsel would telephone and I would send the prisoner to the First Division. These outings are not to exceed 24 hours, but who's counting?... Prisoners did not want to give up the person to be taken to the division. They would resist. They would go arm in arm and resist. I sent a few like that; they would come back all messed up. When it went on like this I started going with the prisoner.... Teams called DAL I and DAL II do the questioning. I saw people blindfolded. They would show me to a room and offer tea, but one heard those voices. I would not know if it was the prisoner I took or someone else. ...I would converse with the prisoner and convey anything he blurted out to the authorities....

"Yes, in the earlier days I was like a German Gestapo prison commander. Prison directorship is not a judicial position. We were only supposed to keep prisoners [and not try them]. But these were all perverted. Everybody in the prison became a commissar. You know the 'Mingle them, make peace between them' rule. I also mingled the leftists and rightists. It didn't work. I put all those on the same trial in the same place. And I was not any worse for it....

78

"We were told that everybody's arms were to be tied when they were taken to court. Once a vehicle on its way to the court was overturned; the prisoners whose arms were tied behind them hurt various parts of their bodies. This would not be allowed even by the Association for the Prevention of Cruelty to Animals...."

Over time Inal, in his words, "softened," and started providing private visits, to develop a dialogue with both the prisoner and his family. He concluded that "to become a prison director requires [education]. Prison directors cannot be made out of soldiers. The soldier's craft is the art of war. Prisons cannot be administered by military orders, using force."

Faik Inal was arrested and charged with violating Article 153 of the Military Penal Code, No. 1632. He was charged with sending prisoner Selcuk Kaya to his father's funeral, sending Aslan Soyyigit with military personnel to the prisoner's father to get wood for the prison, letting prisoner Ramazan Kaya purchase a photocopy machine for the prison, etc. He was also charged with accepting a bribe. He was convicted of misusing his office and sentenced to five months and 25 days and 100,944 TL fine. Since the sentence was less than six months, he could not appeal it and served the sentence at Davutpasa Military Prison.

Reports of unhealthy and inhumane conditions continue to appear in the press:

- A group of lawyers submitted a petition to the Legal Counsel of the First Army in October, pleading that medical attention be afforded to 96 prisoners in Metris Prison. They charged that even in urgent cases there are great delays in receiving medical care. *Ozgurluge*, November, 1986.
- On December 2, 1986, Ilhan Selcuk published in *Cumhuriyet* excerpts from the letter of a man whose son is in prison about the health and nutrition of the prisoners. The father wrote that the daily allocation for food was 260TL a day, a grossly inadequate sum, and that families were forbidden to bring food in from outside. "It is as if the prisoners ... are sentenced to wasting away due to malnutrition.... In the prisons arbitrariness, inhuman practices, mental and physical repression, malnutrition and all kinds of ill-

nesses are ubiquitous. The reaction of the convicts against all these surfaces periodically and is suppressed with noises like, 'they haven't learned their lesson yet.'... It is very difficult for a prisoner to get hospitalized even in cases of emergency."

- A former political prisoner who spent over three years in Metris and Sagmalcilar prisons told us that the allotment for food for prisoners was about 40 cents a day--350 TL. Prisoners got a ladle of soup, chickpeas, beans or lentils, some cracked wheat, spaghetti or rice. Relatives were permitted to send 3,000 TL a week for prisoners to use on food at the prison canteen. A prisoner who had no one to provide money was out of luck. Because the money could come only by mail, prison officials often delayed it, and sometimes kept a percentage for themselves.

- Ertugrul Mavioglu, the former chief editor of the monthly *Cozum*, and three others on trial for membership in a socialist party refused to attend court to protest being handcuffed and chained while being transported to and from court. *Cumhuriyet*, June 3, 1987.

- The General Directorate of Penal and Detention Centers and the Higher Education Council jointly announced that prisoners convicted of common crimes and those charged with but not yet convicted of political crimes could enroll in higher education courses. Prisoners convicted of "anarchical and ideological crimes," however, could not. *Ozgurluge*, November 1986.

- In his October 13, 1986, column in *Cumhuriyet*, Oktay Akbal printed a letter from prison: "We are deprived of many things. Foremost, we are deprived of education. There are a lot of books in the library--we have asked for them numerous times and been denied. They also appropriate books that we order from outside ... You can bring anything into the prison, but never books. They consider books more harmful than anything else. They fear books .... We wish these people would be concerned with us, the young people in the prisons."

- A group of parents of inmates of Mamak Military Prison marched from Kizilay Square to the General Staff Building on January 21, 1987, to submit a petition to the army chief demanding their children have separate cells from those who disagree with their political views. They said that right-wing and left-wing prisoners at Mamak were kept in the same cells together and that frequent clashes take place because of opposing political views. During a confrontation on January 15, one of the inmates, Erdogan Genc, was seriously injured. *Info-Turk*, February 1987.

- Minister of Justice Oltan Sungurlu denied in January that Adana and Mersin prisons were damp and infested with rats. *Cumhuriyet*, January 28, 1987.

- In March a group of parents and relatives of political prisoners, in a petition addressed to the Minister of Justice, said that prison conditions violated all rules of hygiene and were incompatible with human dignity. They said prisoners were kept in cells invaded by snakes and rats and were chained when taken to a hospital. *Info-Turk*, May 1987.

Halil Berktay, one of the panelists arrested by police for taking part in a panel on "Intra-Party Democracy in Socialist Parties," discussed earlier, described to us his detention in Ankara Central Closed Prison:

> We spent our first night in isolation in a special cell block for new-comers, a filthy and unpleasant place with mice running around, before being sent to a ward. The prison is very old--no central heating. The ward is a long hall with bunks on either side, tables down the middle, and one stove in the center which is supposed to heat the whole ward on two buckets of coal; the conditions are very harsh by western standards.

The Human Rights Association has taken on the issue of prison conditions and is increasingly active in publicizing its findings:

- The HRA issued a press release on January 15, 1987, concerning the water used for drinking and washing at Bartin Prison. Relatives of inmates at Bartin had contacted the HRA saying that prisoners were becoming sick from drinking water. The HRA asked the Institute of Environmental Health of the Department of Public Health and the Central Council of the Turkish Medical Association to subject samples of the water to bacteriological and chemical analysis. The water was found to contain coliform bacteria and was said to be "unfit for drinking or other use." After the Minister of Justice received the HRA's report, he told the press that the same water was being used by 25,000 people in Bartin and did not pose a health hazard.

- In May the HRA reported that prisoners were allowed only one bath a year in some prisons, that prisoners are still beaten and placed in sewage water, and that "one of the directors of Mamak Prison testified in court that he ordered newcomers clubbed, and nothing was done about him." *Nokta*, May 3, 1987.

- HRA president Nevzat Helvaci told us in Ankara that the HRA had prepared a report on prison conditions in April. Because they were not permitted to go into the prisons, they talked with people who had been released and evaluated letters from people who are still in prison. They also used information from the few news reports published on prison conditions. In its report the HRA compared Turkish prisons with the United Nations standards on prisons, and concluded that not one Turkish prison meets UN standards. The association asked authorities to take the necessary measures to correct the situation; as yet it had received no reply.

Prison authorities often delay or confiscate mail going in or out of prisons:

- Nevzat Celik, 27, a poet who has been in Metris Prison for over eight years as a defendant in a mass Dev-Sol (Revolutionary Left) case that is still going on, went on a 22-day hunger strike in April to protest the confiscation of his correspondence. The strike was publicized in the Turkish and foreign press; the authorities then promised to deliver his mail regularly and to send him to the hospital for treatment of various health problems. In Istanbul we learned that the authorities had reneged on their promises: Celik was not sent to a hospital and his mail has been interrupted again.
- Prison officials have also confiscated mail sent to Recep Marasli, a 29-year-old publisher now in Diyarbakir Prison who was sentenced to 36 years for publishing six or seven books on the Kurds.

Although the Turkish government has on occasion permitted some delegations of European parliamentarians to visit its prisons, it continues to refuse to permit the International Committee of the Red Cross to do so; surely any serious effort to improve prison conditions should include such visits. In August, however, according to the *Turkish Daily News*, September 4, 1987, the government opened up the prisons to Turkish journalists. Reporters visited Gaziantep L-type Prison on August 18, Sagmalcilar Prison on August 22 and

Bartin Prison in late August; their findings on hunger strikes and prison conditions were reported in the Turkish press.

Hunger Strikes

Hunger strikes continue to be used by prisoners to try to effect change in the prisons. Some have succeeded in improving conditions, but people have died in the process.

- A young man who spent five and a half years in Metris prison as a defendant in the Dev-Sol (Revolutionary Left) case, gave us the names of four prisoners who died during hunger strikes at Metris between March and July 1984:

  Abdullah Meral -- died on 63rd day of strike
  Haydar Basbag -- died on 65th day
  Mehmet Fatih Oktulmus -- died on 65th day
  Hasan Telci -- died on 75th and last day of strike.

  These four and other prisoners had gone on a hunger strike to acquire the legal status of political prisoners, to secure a more democratic life in prison, to resist physical mistreatment, not to be made to behave like a soldier.
- An ex-convict who spent five years in Diyarbakir Prison told us that seven people died there between January and March of 1984, either by fasting or by burning themselves to death to protest torture. The names of four are: Necmettin Buyukkaya, Remzi Ayturk, Orhan Keskin and Yilmaz Demir. The 1984 hunger strike lasted 45 days, after which the prison administration agreed to end beatings and torture.
- In Istanbul we met with a young woman who had spent five and a half years in Metris Prison. "While I was in Metris I took part in a hunger strike--it was a death fast. At the end of two months I was in bad shape--I was dying; three of my friends had already died. The doctors had never intervened, but suddenly a doctor came and gave me an injection and took me to the hospital, and I gradually recovered. I couldn't understand why the doctors intervened, until later when my mother told me that it was just at that point that Helsinki Watch had begun to make inquiries about me.

83

The Turkish press frequently prints reports about hunger strikes in prisons throughout Turkey:

- Sixty-one detainees kept in observation wards in Adana Prison went on a hunger strike to protest maltreatment, inadequate exercise periods, restrictions on family visits, inadequate food and lack of access to books. Prisoners of Kurdish origin protested that their parents, though they did not speak Turkish, were not allowed to speak to them in Kurdish during their visits. Minister of Justice Oltan Sungurlu denounced the strike as "ideological," and a "cover-up for other things." *Cumhuriyet*, February 18 through 23, 1987.

- Four death row inmates ended a ten day hunger strike at Sinop prison; three were reported to be in good condition--Ahmet Erman, Hayati Ozkan and Ergun Aydas. A fourth, Nazim Silaci, was under treatment at Sinop Ataturk Hospital. *Cumhuriyet*, May 12, 1987.

- Eleven political prisoners were continuing their week-long hunger strike, undertaken to protest participating in the national anthem ceremony held twice a week, wearing uniforms and having their hair cut in prison style. *Cumhuriyet*, April 28, 1987.

- A group of inmates at Ankara Prison started a hunger strike to protest the death of prisoner Ahmet Cetin, alleging that Cetin's treatment for kidney insufficiency was delayed at the medical ward because he was a leftist convict. An Ankara prosecutor's aide denied charges that Cetin's body had traces of beatings. Nevzat Helvaci, the president of the Human Rights Association, said the death was caused by negligence; "if Cetin had been treated on time he would not have died. He was not sick when he entered prison." *Cumhuriyet*, March 19, 1987.

In recent months the press has reported hunger strikes against ill-treatment in a number of other prisons, including Bursa, Mersin, Nigde, Metris, Bartin, Izmir and Amasya. On July 23rd the *Turkish Daily News* reported that hunger strikes started by 246 prisoners in Malatya and 24 in Sagmalcilar had been joined by over 400 prisoners in Metris Military Prison. The prisoners were demanding better and more decent living conditions and an end to the beating of prisoners and the use of solitary confinement, restrictions on family visits, and bans on newspapers, books, radios, and correspondence. According to

Info-Turk, July and August, 1987, more than two thousand political prisoners have staged hunger strikes in military and civilian prisons since July 8, 1987.

According to an Associated Press report of August 10, 1987, a group of families of prisoners carried out a two-day hunger strike to support the prisoners' hunger strikes demanding better prison conditions. About 40 family members, most of them women, started the strike at Guven Park in downtown Ankara in 97 degree weather after their request to see Minister of Justice Oltan Sungurlu had been turned down. The families also asked for increased contact with the prisoners: "We are allowed to see them for only fifteen minutes behind a glass wall every two weeks," said Cavidan Kocacari, a spokesperson for the group.

According to the *Turkish Daily News*, August 3, 1987, Minister of Justice Oltan Sungurlu, meeting with the press in Bursa in August, said that recent incidents of torture, hunger strikes and beatings were normal: "Such incidents have always taken place in Turkish prisons and they will occur in the future. In a democratic environment such happenings should be considered normal." Sungurlu went on to say that prisoners were deliberately complaining about living conditions and that there was no way to improve things. "They know this themselves but they ignore that fact and seek ways of influencing public opinion. ... Many prisoners are involved in politics ... and are eager to continue their ideological battle even in state prisons."

In its September 5-6, 1987 issue, however, the *Turkish Daily News* reported that Minister Sungurlu had acknowledged that "some of the complaints of prisoners are justified," and that his ministry would try to improve the situation. He said that prisoners' food allowances would be increased but that restrictions on visits depended on the physical restrictions in prison space. He said it was not possible to allow radios or cassette players, as electronic equipment had been used "to contact the international community." He also said that bringing clothes and food would continue to be prohibited, as "the practice had been exploited in the past." It was "up to the prison authorities whether or not to allow warm clothes brought in from outside in the winter." Sungurlu said he was "sad to read about the terrible conditions of bathrooms, toilets and kitchens in some prisons" and stated that this showed that the ministry's inspection system was not good enough to detect this fact.

Association of Families of Detainees and Convicts

In Istanbul we attended a panel discussion on prison conditions organized by the Association of Families of Detainees and Convicts (described earlier in *Freedom of Association*). Four speakers--three relatives of prisoners and one doctor--presented harrowing pictures of the conditions that led to the hunger strikes, the effects of the strikes and the actions of prison authorities and some doctors.

> "We relatives supported the strikes," said one speaker, discussing the hunger strikes in 1984. "President Evren said they were just pretending, no one was dying. A few days later the deaths began; with the first death the authorities got scared. Then two more died on the 66th day. On the 74th day a fourth died--then a dialogue began.... The four who died were a soldier, a student, a worker and a porter. In their last letters they said they were happy to die, rather than dying a little every day."

> Another speaker, the brother of a striker, described getting special permission to see his brother on the 62nd or 63rd day of the strike: "I was the only one permitted to go there; my brother couldn't see me. I said, 'do you recognize my voice?' His life was gone from his face--he didn't look human. He was angry that I had gotten special permission from the General Staff to come. He said, 'Why did they separate me from my friends?' I started beating the walls--I was insane. I wanted to speak to the chief of the hospital; the chief surgeon, a general, met me. I said 'give them their rights.' He said, 'they're going to be executed anyway; if we give them serum they'll throw it out. There's nothing I can do.'" The strike ended after that, and his brother survived.

Prison Visits

Restrictions on prison visits continue to be a source of conflict between prisoners and prison authorities, both in the length of the visits and in the conditions imposed on prisoners and visitors. A prisoner's sister told us she is permitted to see her brother only once a week for 15 minutes; "I can't see his face properly, and I have to talk to him through a telephone." A former prisoner at Diyarbakir was permitted to see his family once a week, "sometimes for as short a time as one minute or two minutes--if a visit was as long as five minutes, I was happy." His meetings with his lawyer were just as short. "Prison officials used to say, 'you dare not speak too long with your lawyer; as soon as the private hits your leg, get up and leave.' There were no limits on the number of visits our lawyers could make, but most of them could only last one or two minutes, and we were warned not to speak about prison conditions."

Prisoners have also protested that only husbands and wives, sisters and brothers and parents are allowed to visit, but not cousins, uncles and aunts, nieces and nephews or friends.

Improvements in Prison Conditions

Prison conditions have improved markedly in one respect: beatings and torture, which continue in interrogation centers and police stations, apparently are much less frequent in prisons. Former prisoners, lawyers for current and former inmates, as well as politicians and academics told us that the changes took place in 1984 and 1985. Various explanations were given: hunger strikes by prisoners that caused bad publicity, visits by European parliamentarians, reports on prison conditions issued by Amnesty International and Helsinki Watch, the general improvement in political conditions in Turkey, and Turkey's efforts to become a full member of the European Community.

- Halil Berktay was told by long-term prisoners in Ankara Central Prison that political prisoners who were there between 1981 and 1984 suffered severe repression: continual beatings, attacks by warders, insults and humiliations. This treatment ended in 1984, partly as a result of the general improvement in national political conditions, and partly as a result of resistance by prisoners in Ward 4.

87

- According to Emil Galip Sandalci, president of the Istanbul section of the Human Rights Association, conditions in Metris Prison have improved in the last few months, comparatively speaking. Strip searches before visits have stopped; prisoners' heads are no longer shaved; there are TVs in the wards, but no radios. Sandalci knew of one case of beating of a prisoner; the army guard responsible was sent away to another unit. Prisoners continue to ask for longer visiting hours and to complain about mail delays and confiscations.

- A former prisoner at Metris Prison told us that the worst period was the time from 1983 to 1985; there has been no radical change since then, but relative improvement. There are fewer beatings than before, arbitrary prohibitions against family or attorney visits are rarer. He ascribes these improvements to resistance by prisoners and relatives and to public opinion.

- Kenan Nehrozoglu, a member of Parliament from Mardin who served on the Parliamentary Commission on Prison Conditions that issued a report in 1985, told us that nothing had happened as a direct result of the report. He said, however, that "prison conditions are better now: there used to be daily beatings of prisoners in military prisons--now there are few--and the food is better. These changes are due to visits by members of Parliament and others that came about because of complaints in the newspapers and in Parliament."

- A young woman who was released after spending five years as a political prisoner in Metris Prison agreed that conditions had changed there--she dated it to the period after the winter of 1984-85. "During my first years in prison people were beaten regularly; now they are not beaten at all. Step by step conditions have gotten better--the hunger strikes helped people hear us. And we were helped by the changes in the political situation in Turkey and by the efforts of groups like Helsinki Watch and others. We could feel the visits of outsiders--you could smell it in the atmosphere of the prison, that something extra was happening outside."

Diyarbakir Prison

In Diyarbakir Prison, one of the worst prisons in Turkey, conditions have also apparently improved since 1984. Prisoners are not routinely beaten and tortured, as they had been in the past. Because almost all of the prisoners

88

in Diyarbakir are Kurds, and because many problems in Diyarbakir are specifically related to the Kurdish issue, a detailed report on the prison will be found in the section on *The Kurdish Minority*.

Death Sentences

The death penalty remains in the Turkish penal code, and two convicts have been executed since the election of the Ozal government--both were hanged in 1984. Turkish law provides that death sentences must be ratified by Parliament. As of August 10, 1987, 153 death sentences were awaiting review by Parliament. Of these, 77 involve leftists, 17 involve rightists, 55 have been convicted of common crimes, and four are Palestinian guerrillas involved in a raid on the Egyptian Embassy in Ankara in 1979. According to *Info-Turk*, May 1987, at least 21 of the death sentences have been given to PKK militants.

The Democratic Left Party has submitted a draft bill to Parliament to abolish capital punishment; the bill has remained with the Parliamentary Justice Commission for over a year. The Social Democratic People's Party (SHP) is against the death penalty in principle, and has suggested that the issue be taken up at the time the new penal code is reviewed; the proposed penal code does not end the death penalty. According to the *Turkish Daily News*, March 3-9, 1987, Prime Minister Ozal notified the Parliamentary Justice Commission in February that "lifting the death penalty is not possible under present circumstances."

The Turkish Medical Association opposes capital punishment; in October 1985 the group submitted a statement advocating abolition of the death penalty to the President, the Prime Minister and members of Parliament. As a result, six members of the executive board were tried on charges of violating the Law on Associations that prohibits any interference in politics. In September 1986 they were acquitted.

The Union of Turkish Bar Associations also opposes the death penalty. At a conference in April 1987, the group stated:

> The General Assembly of the Union of Turkish Bars repeats its view that the death penalty is no longer acceptable today and stresses the necessity to ratify the Sixth Protocol on abolition of the death penalty, which has been accepted by the

Council of Europe, and to remove this punishment from our laws which is incompatible with human dignity.

On September 19, 1987, the Human Rights Association opened a campaign to abolish the death penalty.

According to Amnesty International, public opinion in Turkey appears to be in favor of the death penalty, and the government is strongly committed to it. In a speech in Mus on October 3, 1984, President Evren supported the execution of terrorists:

> Some of the wanted anarchists fire at gendarmerie--jeeps that return from duty at night and make an officer and a soldier a martyr. Now, shall I send him to court after I capture him and not execute him? Shall I look after him for a life-time? Should the traitor who has raised his weapon against the "brave soldiers" who shed their blood for this country be looked after for years and years? Can you accept this? *Cumhuriyet*, October 4, 1984. (For a fuller discussion of this issue, see "The Death Penalty in Turkey," Amnesty International, June 1, 1987.)

V. THE KURDISH MINORITY

Destruction of Ethnic Identity

The Kurds have never had a country of their own, although they lay claim to a large geographic area that they call Kurdistan and have shared a common language, religion and culture for thousands of years. The oil-rich, mountainous region that the Kurds call Kurdistan was carved up after World War I and parcelled out to Turkey, Iran and Iraq. Kurds are now living in all of those countries and, in smaller numbers, in Syria and the USSR.

No one knows precisely how many Kurds there are in the world today, although the figure of nearly 20 million often appears in the press. The British-based Minority Rights Group, which has been reporting on the Kurds since 1975, says that in 1980 the total Kurdish population in the world was 16,320,000, of which 8,455,000 were in Turkey. Most people estimate the number of Kurds in Turkey at the present time at 8 to 10 million, although some estimates are as high as 15 million. No official census of Kurds is taken, since the government refuses to acknowledge that there are Kurds in Turkey.

The Kurds in Turkey are severely repressed, a repression that dates back in modern times to Ataturk and the establishment of the Turkish Republic in 1923. Since then the Turkish government has spent considerable energy to repress, displace or assimilate its Kurds. After the 1980 military coup, thousands of Kurdish activists and sympathizers--many of them not involved in violence-- were thrown into Diyarbakir Prison, known as one of the worst prisons in the world.

The Kurdish issue is so sensitive in Turkey that it is only recently that it has been discussed at all in the press. Hasan Cemal of *Cumhuriyet* confirmed this to us in June 1987, saying that the Kurdish question is not covered in any real sense; he said that the press feels constrained, and that it will take some time before journalists can really discuss the issue. As described earlier in

91

Regions Populated by the Kurds

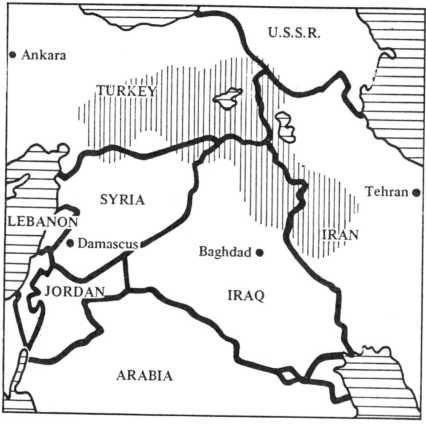

| | Regions inhabited by the Kurdish Nation

Freedom of the Press, it is only in recent months that the press has even been able to use the word "Kurd" in relation to Kurds in Turkey.

Taboos against discussing the Kurdish situation extend to secure members of the establishment: members of Parliament and political leaders told us that we could quote them on any subject--torture, police brutality, prison conditions, political developments--any subject except the Kurds. A political leader told us that it would be twenty years before the Kurdish question could be dealt with openly and honestly. A member of Parliament cannot stand up on the floor of Parliament and suggest that there is a Kurdish problem. When a member of the SHP recently suggested openly that the party's platform be printed in Kurdish as well as in Turkish, he was removed from his party post and his case sent to the disciplinary committee of the SHP. Although no action had been taken yet when we visited Turkey in June, several SHP leaders said that if he were not expelled from the party, the party itself might be forced to disband.

Attempts to destroy the Kurds' ethnic identity take many forms: the Kurdish language, although often the only language spoken in parts of the east, is frequently not permitted in official settings (see Appendices 4 and 5); Kurdish music and dance are also forbidden (see Appendix 6); a Kurdish couple cannot give their child a Kurdish name; no books or journals can be printed in Kurdish; the Kurdish New Year cannot be celebrated. It is ironic that the Turkish government's treatment of the Kurds closely resembles the policies of the Bulgarian government towards its ethnic Turks, policies that the Turkish government has vehemently -- and quite properly -- condemned. (See *Destroying Ethnic Identity: The Turks of Bulgaria*, Helsinki Watch, September 1987.)

Repression of the Kurds affects well-known and ordinary people alike. Serafettin Elci, a former Member of Parliament, was asked in Parliament whether he was a Turk or a Kurd; he answered, "I am a Kurd." In 1981 he was tried for that statement and sentenced to two years and three months at hard labor. Ibrahim Tatlises, one of Turkey's most popular singers, was recently charged and tried for using a Kurdish phrase at a concert in Sweden; he could have been sentenced to 24 years. The charges were dismissed after Tatlises indicated his remorse.

93

The following examples illustrate the pervasiveness of the government's policies:

- Ten officials of the State Institute of Statistics were tried before the State Security Court on the charge of "separatism" for listing the Kurdish language under the heading of "What languages do you speak?" on forms used in the 1980 and 1985 censuses. The state prosecutor accused them of listing "a dialect of the Turkish language" as a distinct language. *Info-Turk,* June 1986. The defendants were eventually acquitted.

- Ismail Gaya, a teacher in the village school in Kolak, in Denizli, was tried for saying, "I am the son of a Kurd. I was born a Kurd and I will die a Kurd." He had shouted this during an argument with another teacher who upset him by slapping students for giggling during the recital of the national anthem on May 2, 1986. The State Security Court acquitted him, deciding that he had not uttered the words with malice. *Cumhuriyet,* October 24, 1986.

- Edip Servet Demirci, former Vice-General Secretary of the SHP, was arrested in Yalova, a seaside resort on the Marmara Sea, and brought to Ankara for questioning in relation to charges that he had been speaking Kurdish at the SHP headquarters in Ankara. Demirci was held for one day in Ankara and later questioned by State Security Court Prosecutor Ulku Coskun. *Ozgurluge,* September 1986.

- A tourist guide, Ersin Konuk, in the small resort town of Kusadasi was charged with separatism for being in possession of a map of the Ottoman Empire printed before 1911 in Germany that designated East Anatolia as "Ermenistan" (Armenia) and Southeast Anatolia as "Kurdistan." A sentence of 15 years was asked. *Ozgurluge,* November 1986.

- Ahmet Turk, a former member of parliament, was detained with three relatives and subsequently charged with possessing a separatist video cassette which had been found in the garbage outside his house. *Cumhuriyet,* February 11, 1987. He was still in custody at the time of our visit in June.

- Mustafa Ustun, chief of police in Bitlis demanded that charges be brought against twelve people who had given their children Kurdish names. The Ankara prosecutor referred the matter to the Ministry of the Interior; two officials reported that the names were not Turkish and violated Law No. 1587, article 16/4, which states that names that contradict the national culture, morality and traditions, and insult the public cannot be legally registered on birth certificates. Mehmet Seref Kocaman was summoned to court, where he was forced to change the names of his children. Four other fathers were tried for the same offense. *Nokta*, February 15, 1987. (See Appendix 7 for a copy of a Turkish District Court order changing the names of two children.)

- Marie Annick Lanternier, a member of the French medical team, Medecins sans Frontieres, was imprisoned for eight months in 1982 for possessing Kurdish music tapes. *Le Quotidien de Paris*, January 25, 1982.
- Franz Reissig, a German employee in the Istanbul office of Lufthansa, was arrested in 1983 for photographing an advertisement featuring an antique globe on which was written "Kurdistan." *The Guardian*, March 23, 1983.
- Turkish authorities have changed the names of many Kurdish villages. On May 25, 1986, *Tercuman* reported that the names of four of every five villages--2,842 of 3,524 villages in the provinces of Adiyaman, Gaziantep, Urfa, Mardin, Siirt and Diyarbakir--had been changed.

The ban on things Kurdish affects non-Kurds as well. Turks have gone to prison for defending the rights of Kurds.

- Ismail Besikci, a Turkish sociologist, and Recep Marasli, a Turkish publisher, have both served long terms in prison for writing and publishing about the Kurds. Besikci was released in May 1987. Marasli is still in Diyarbakir Prison, serving a 36-year sentence.

Kurds who have emigrated from Turkey find that the long arm of Turkish injustice has followed them even abroad.

- The Turkish Embassy protested when Emin Bozarslan, a Kurdish refugee in Denmark, tried to open a course in Copenhagen instructing teachers in the Kurdish language.
- The Turkish Embassy in Sweden objected to the establishment in Stockholm of Kurdish day care centers. The Turkish Embassy in Germany tells German officials not to accept Kurdish names for children born in Germany.

- The Turkish Embassy in the United States protested to the Cathedral of St. John the Divine in New York when it opened an exhibition of photographs of Kurdistan.
- The Turkish Embassy in Canada refused to issue legal forms to a Kurdish refugee who had become a Canadian citizen until he erased "Kurdish" and substituted "Turkish" in answer to a question about his mother tongue.

A Kurdish lawyer in Ankara told us that he had given his son a Kurdish name. The Bureau of Population Statistics made him change the child's name in order to get a birth certificate. He said, sadly, "Everyone has the right to be a human being. One cannot renege on those rights. But Kurds in Turkey don't have their natural rights--they are denied, because according to the official ideology, there is no such thing as a Kurd in Turkey; everyone is Turkish."

Diyarbakir Prison

According to former inmates and lawyers who have represented hundreds of prisoners in Diyarbakir Prison, conditions in the prison, once known as the worst prison in Turkey and one of the worst prisons in the world, have improved in some respects since 1984. Although we traveled to Diyarbakir, we were not able to see this for ourselves; the government would not permit us to visit the prison, despite formal requests to the relevant ministries that we began several months before our trip.

Diyarbakir Prison is a military remand center that houses as many as 1,000 detainees, most of whom are Kurds. Prisoners remain in the prison while they are on trial; once convicted, they are sent elsewhere to serve their sentences. Because of the length of many trials, particularly the mass political trials, some prisoners have remained for many years in Diyarbakir where they have been subjected to vile forms of torture. Lawyers described to us how detainees came to court with swollen faces and downcast eyes, having been forced by their torturers to sign false papers stating that their injuries predated their arrests. Those who dared complain to the unresponsive judges were beaten up again as soon as they left the courtroom. Prisoners who were convicted often chose not

96

to appeal because that would entail more time in Diyarbakir rather than serving their sentences elsewhere.

The stories we heard about Diyarbakir were sickening: a man forced to eat a live rat (it appears in the court records); a well-known defense lawyer who was himself arrested, brutally tortured in the prison and pulled around by a rope tied to his penis; prisoners put in septic tanks as punishment, forced to eat excrement and drink urine. The government admits to 32 deaths in the prison between 1981 and 1984; unofficial sources put the count at 67, including several prisoners who burned themselves alive rather than endure further abuse.

In Diyarbakir we met with three lawyers who have represented hundreds of prisoners. They all agreed that conditions have improved in Diyarbakir since 1984, the result of mass hunger strikes and the resulting international attention. Long-term prisoners are no longer routinely beaten and tortured, but many problems remain.

The prisoners who have been taken to Diyarbakir Prison in recent years are a different sort -- most of them are peasants accused of sympathizing with terrorists and giving them food and supplies. Often these peasants have been picked up with all the members of their families, and beaten, tortured and abused by gendarmes in order to get information from them or simply to intimidate them. Many of these people have been subsequently released and have described the tortures to which they were subjected, including *falaka*, suspension and electric shocks. Most effective, apparently, is the threat of torture against other family members: "I was ready to confess that I had killed 100 men," a former detainee reported, "because they brought in my wife and sister, stripped them and threatened to rape them right there." After torture at the gendarmerie station, some peasants are charged and taken to Diyarbakir Prison; there they are routinely given a preliminary "training session"--beatings that can last as long as a day.

Ahmet Karak (not his real name), a lawyer, has represented many Diyarbakir inmates since the 1980 coup; his sources of information are his clients, whom he sees two or three times a week, prison staff and prisoners' declarations in court. He described the situation in Diyarbakir, both before and after 1984:

Systematic torture began in Diyarbakir Prison in 1981. This torture--it's not possible to explain, even by a person who sees it. One prisoner, Remzi Ercanlar, a defendant in the TIKKO case (Turkish Labor and Peasant Salvation Army), was forced to eat a live rat--you can read about it in the official court papers. Prisoners were kept in septic tanks full of excrement, and taken to toilets where excrement was smeared on their faces; people were made to eat excrement and drink urine. Many people died and many lost their minds or their health. Official reports say that 32 died in the prison; according to people who lived there, 67 died between 1981 and 1984.

In 1984 torture in interrogation centers did not stop, but torture in prison stopped. This was due to several factors: first, opposition by prisoners that took the form of hunger strikes and other actions, like refusing to go to visits of relatives--the relatives became very disturbed and made an issue of prison conditions. Second, pressure from the European Parliament and Amnesty International. Third, Evren's and Ozal's declaration that Turkey would be a democratic country. Fourth, every time the Turkish government went to Europe it met with opposition because of torture in Turkey; this was especially true when Turkey wanted to take the issue of the Bulgarian Turks to Europe.

It's hard to compare conditions before 1984 and after 1984-- they are so much better. Prisoners' resistance led to changing the entire staff of the prison; no one from the pre-1984 staff is left. When the conditions changed the prisoners thought they were living in heaven. Now their complaints are that there is not enough food--for a ward of 50 people, food for only 30 is provided--and they cannot get the books they want.

According to civil law in Turkey, nephews and nieces are 'relatives,' but in prison only parents, husbands or wives, brothers and sisters are allowed to visit--no uncles or aunts. Before if your surname was the same, you could visit a prisoner. The change was made to isolate the prisoners from the world.

Some new prisoners, mostly Kurdish peasants who are accused of helping the PKK, are tortured when they first come
to Diyarbakir. But mostly it's a question of psychological
pressure on prisoners, and not physical torture.

Another Diyarbakir attorney, Mehmet Keskin (not his real name), confirmed Ahmet Karak's conclusions about improvements in Diyarbakir. Keskin
has handled political cases and has many lawyer friends who represent Diyarbakir inmates.

Hasan Isik (not his real name), a third lawyer from Diyarbakir,
described conditions as better since 1984 because of the prisoners' fasting and
protests: "By that, I mean it's not the best prison in Turkey, but it's relatively
better. During the protests, the prisoners had one wish--they wanted to be
treated like human beings." Isik continued:

Diyarbakir is still not an ordinary jail. For example, if you are
in prison in Malatya you have no problems about food, and
you can have any publications you want. And you don't have
to sing martial songs--in Diyarbakir you used to have to know
36 martial songs by heart; now it's only one martial song, the
Turkish liberation march. But you have to pray before eating.
In Malatya there is no national march and no prayer.
There's still a problem with food--people are given dried
beans without meat. Also, the people who went on hunger
strikes should be fed better than the others--milk and healthy
foods--but they are not allowed to eat more. The other
prisoners try to help them, but they are not allowed.
New prisoners are still being beaten when they first arrive.
They are taken to a room and given new clothes and then
beaten by guards for not more than one day--sometimes only
for hours. If they respond badly to the guards, the guards do
falaka on them. These are called "training sessions." Before
1984 the "training sessions" were much longer.

In Istanbul we met with Kenan Simsek (a pseudonym), 31, who spent
four years in Diyarbakir Prison. He was arrested in 1979, when police raided
his house in Ankara and found leftist publications, including copies of books by
Ismail Besikci about the Kurds. In March 1980 he was sent to Diyarbakir:

Before the coup there was no considerable mistreatment in Diyarbakir; the repression began after the coup. First they shut the doors from the wards to the gardens, then the doors from one dormitory to another, so that each dormitory was isolated. Then visiting hours were reduced from 15 or 20 minutes to three to five minutes. Prisoners were forced to stand and salute when guards came in, and we had to sing a national hymn each morning. We tried to resist this treatment on the grounds that we were not military personnel, but political prisoners. Then they began to sentence people to solitary confinement in order to break their resistance, and some wards were denied visits from relatives.

Things got much better in 1984, after we had a hunger strike that lasted 45 days. Prison authorities agreed to stop the beating and torture--and with this, the beating and torture stopped. I was released in October 1984, but I know from friends who were released later that it ended. There were some single incidents--some people who were caught at the border were brought to prison and we heard their cries from torture; we protested again and the mistreatment stopped. Gradually, starting in 1984, all the staff was replaced. The two main torturers, specially trained persons, Ali Osman Aydin and Esat Oktay Yildirim, were replaced after four people died in hunger strikes.

Although the torture stopped, prisoners still could not go outside for fresh air. Then there was a visit from the European Council--prisoners were allowed to go outside, and wards were given TV sets--and these things continued after the visitors left. If the situation was relatively improved in Turkey, it was because of the solidarity of people like the Council of Europe and Helsinki Watch.

Recently reports about conditions at Diyarbakir Prison have begun surfacing in the Turkish press. In the July 12-18, 1987, issue of *2000'e Dogru*, for example, a long article describes the torture and humiliation inflicted on Diyarbakir prisoners between 1980 and 1984. The article details nightmarish tortures: prisoners beaten on the soles of their feet or their buttocks until they fainted; made to crawl in the courtyard until their arms bled; forced to plunge their heads into sewage water full of excrement; forced to eat part of a dead mouse.

To protest these terrible conditions, four prisoners -- Ferhat Kuntay, Mahmut Zengin, Esref Anyik and Necmi Oner -- piled up papers, cotton from beds, and pieces of cloth, poured flammable liquid over the pile, and set fire to it. *2000'e Dogru* quoted another prisoner who said: "Ferhat Kuntay said, 'We sacrifice ourselves for the people in prison, we burn ourselves in this prison, we burn ourselves to death in order to bring human living conditions. This must be known.' And then he set his head on fire." All four burned themselves to death.

The article names the prison commanders responsible for the beatings and torture. It also describes the deaths by beating of several prisoners: Abdurrahman Cecen and Ibis Uras, beaten to death in the "entrance cells;" Ali Evek, a hunger striker kicked to death by Inner Security Commander Esat Oktay Yildiran in 1981; M. Emin Akpinar beaten to death by a sergeant because he did not speak Turkish and could not memorize the required 56 marches -- his death was called "natural" in the medical report.

We were told that prisoners who insist on their Kurdish identity suffer additional mistreatment: prisoners in Diyarbakir Prison are punished if they speak Kurdish, sing in Kurdish or perform Kurdish dances. Several people--lawyers and former prisoners--told us of parents who visited children in prison but could not speak to them because they knew no Turkish and were not allowed to speak Kurdish. We were told of mothers gazing at their imprisoned sons through the visitor screens, tears streaming down their cheeks, forced to remain mute. Lawyers told us of the impossibility of defending a client who spoke no Turkish--because they were not allowed to converse in Kurdish, they had no way of finding out the barest facts in the case, making their representation pure farce.

Kenan Simsek, the former prisoner quoted above, described his experiences as a Kurd in Diyarbakir:

I was arrested in 1979; police raided my house and found leftist publications and many copies of books about the Kurds by

101

Ismail Besikci.... The first time we were collectively beaten, as a whole ward, was in December 1980, because we spoke Kurdish and sang Kurdish songs. Also, we had to go through corridors with soldiers on the left and right who beat us with truncheons--this happened whenever we were taken to solitary confinement, or to individual cells.

Prison discipline is aimed at furthering the government's program of assimilation. A former prisoner paraphrased a speech by the prison commander: "You are Turks. You will forget Kurdish. This is a school for you; you will be educated as Kemalist youth. We should destroy you, but the Turkish Army will educate you instead and make you fit for society. You must act like soldiers. When you see military personnel, you must salute and march in military fashion."

Guerrilla Attacks in the Southeast

Since 1984 militant Kurdish separatists have been carrying on guerrilla warfare in southeast Turkey. Kurdish guerrillas come down from mountain caves or from bases across the Syrian or Iraqi borders and attack small villages, usually at night, where they shoot and kill village guards and civilians they believe to be cooperating with Turkish authorities. Then they escape by crossing back over the borders or hiding in caves. Newsweek, March 30, 1987, described Turkey as the site of "the world's most bitter guerrilla war." Some Turkish officials, quoted in The Christian Science Monitor, July 27, 1987, described the guerrilla warfare as "the most serious threat" Turkey has experienced in the last fifty years.

Terrorism has accelerated in recent months: according to the Ankara Domestic Service, June 21, 1987, on June 20, terrorists attacked Pinarcik village in Mardin near the Syrian border, clashed with village guards, attacked houses with hand grenades and Molotov cocktails and fired on women and children who were trying to flee the burning houses--eight men, six women and sixteen children were killed. On July 8, 28 people, eleven of them children, were killed in two other Mardin villages; four more, including a three-month-old baby, were killed in the village of Kirimh on July 9. In Mardin there have been incidents in which military personnel have been killed when their vehicles have driven over landmines.

The death toll has been dreadful: in July 1987 the *Turkish Daily News* reported the three-year death toll at 715: 289 civilians, most of whom were women and children, 159 military personnel, and 267 terrorists, reportedly killed in shootouts with security forces. On August 10, 1987, the *Turkish Daily News* reported the official figures as 500 soldiers and villagers and 290 terrorists killed since 1984. There have been many incidents since then, including one in Siirt in which 25 people, 14 of them children, were killed by terrorists who first engaged in an armed clash with village guards, and then attacked villagers' homes with firearms and hand grenades. On September 21, 1987, terrorists killed eleven people, including five women and four children, in a small hamlet in Sirnak near the Iraqi border.

Terrorists also kidnap civilians:

- On April 30, 1987, terrorists kidnapped 12 peasants, 15 to 25 years old, from Semdinli in Hakkari province. Four, including the ANAP county chief, escaped and returned to the village. They and nine others were then arrested and imprisoned for not resisting the terrorists. *Cumhuriyet*, June 9, 1987.
- In three incidents in early June, terrorists in Semdinli kidnapped 34 people. Twenty-three were freed by security forces on June 5. *Ankara Anatolia*, June 3, 4, 6 and 8, 1987.
- In late July insurgents abducted 20 villagers from a highland grazing camp near the Iraqi border; 17 were later rescued by security forces. *Turkish Daily News*, August 1-2, 1987.

These terrorist actions are believed to be the work of the PKK, the Marxist-Leninist Kurdish Workers' Party; the party says its aim is to "liberate" the Kurdish-inhabited areas of Turkey and create an independent state. According to *Cumhuriyet*, Feb. 24, 1987, the PKK was founded in 1978 by Abdullah Ocalan, a student at the Faculty of Political Science at Ankara University, and was involved in numerous armed incidents before the September 12, 1980, coup. After the coup, the leaders left the country and reorganized near the borders of Syria and Iraq. In August 1984 the current wave of terrorism began with a terrorist action in Eruh and Semdinli; by the end of 1984 there were raids on military convoys and gendarmerie stations on a regular basis. The raids then extended to small villages that are difficult for security forces to protect. Abdullah Ocalan is believed to be based in Damascus, Syria.

No one knows how many terrorists are carrying on guerrilla warfare in the southeast; we heard estimates ranging from 200 to 1500. Mardin Police Chief Aydin Genc believes there are no more than 200 terrorists, including those who come over the border, and that many of them are 15- and 16-year-old boys. Unal Marasli, the director of the Office of Research in the Foreign Ministry and the only government official with whom we were able to discuss the question, said: "According to our information, there are only 600 or 700 terrorists; but those figures may not be reliable."

After the June and July massacres, the government increased its estimates: according to the *Turkish Daily News*, July 25-26, 1987, during a press conference in Diyarbakir on July 10th, Prime Minister Ozal asserted that the government knew of 3,496 terrorists -- 1,158 active terrorists and 2,338 people who gave them refuge. In an interview that appeared in *Hurriyet* on August 22, 1987, however, Prime Minister Ozal said: "The bandits number 300 or 400 individuals who can exploit the terrain in southeastern Turkey."

The PKK does not generally reveal information about the numbers of its followers; on August 1, 1987, however, a corres pondent from *Gunaydin* was told by PKK militants in Iraq that the PKK has 38 camps and 8,000 armed men in Turkey.

There is also uncertainty about who the terrorists are-- are they Iranian, Iraqi or Syrian Kurds, or are they Kurds from Turkey? Are they Turkish Kurds who have fled across the borders, only to return on hit-and-run terrorist missions? Or are they local Kurds who lead a double life--ordinary peasants during the day, and militant terrorists at night?

According to Unal Marasli of the Foreign Ministry, "Some are Turks, some are not. They are based mostly in Syria, but some are based in Iraq; they are being trained, equipped and supported by someone, but we don't know by whom, or where their weapons are coming from. Most of the people in the southeast don't support them, because they attack civilians--women and children--and try to intimidate the local population."

According to U.S. Ambassador Robert Strausz-Hupe: "The militants constitute a well-orchestrated group of armed men who penetrate the border every day." He and members of his staff believe that it is a case of infiltration, not insurgency, theorizing that if it were an insurgency, there would be more protests in urban areas.

A journalist in Mardin said:

The PKK hide here or go back across the border; they come and go. Some of them come and stay in the mountains; some of them go back to Syria to get supplies. They get financial support from outside, but we don't know from where.

Bulent Ecevit told us: "Most of the terrorism comes from across the border--there is no widespread popular support for the terrorists." This was a view that we heard expressed by nearly everyone with whom we discussed the matter. Suleyman Demirel said, "There is no local support for the terrorists--that's why people are being killed by the separatists. People are afraid of the terrorists; the state doesn't give them enough security and they can't protect themselves." Erdal Inonu, Chairman of the SHP, said: "In general, there is not much popular support for the guerrillas; the situation would have been much worse if people supported them."

According to one member of Parliament from the southeast, however, some significant support for the terrorists exists in the border areas:

In the beginning, the Kurdish people were against the terrorists. Some were sympathetic, but the terrorists started attacking people and taking money from them. When the military took over in 1980, the Kurds were happy. But then the military started getting worse than the terrorists, so now about 40 percent of the villagers in the border areas support the terrorists. But they don't all want a separate state--they just want the freedom to be Kurds.

The Government's Response

In 1985 the Turkish government started military operations against the PKK after terrorists had begun descending on villages for food and torturing and killing villagers who refused to cooperate with them.

Government troops used against the terrorists include the police, the gendarmerie (internal security forces under the authority of the Ministry of the Interior) and special anti-terrorist squads. In addition, the government established a system of village guards--local peasants who were given arms to protect the villages against terrorists.

Conflicting reports on the numbers and kinds of troops involved have appeared in the press. Special operations teams--a total of 1,500 men specially trained in guerrilla warfare by the General Directorate of Police--were reported by *Milliyet* in December 1986 to be preparing to combat terrorism in the area. Commando units under control of the Second and Seventh Armies are also operating in the southeast. *The Anatolia News Agency* reported in July that the Security Department had sent over 1,300 anti- terrorist troops to the southeast.

The Christian Science Monitor reported on July 27, 1987:

A special, well-trained, well-equipped "strike force," probably numbering 5,000, will be formed to fight the terrorists in place of regular Army units. Army officers in the region have complained that regular soldiers doing military service are not properly trained nor equipped to deal with terrorism.

According to *Hurriyet*, August 12, 1987, a "Public Security Army Corps," commanded by Lt. Gen. Hulusi Sayin, has been set up to "break the back" of the separatist terrorists in southeastern Anatolia. The 25,000 man army corps will deal with terrorism only in the eight southeastern provinces; servicemen who have been trained as commandos and have had success in combatting terrorism will be selected. According to *Hurriyet*, "Military units operating against the separatists have found it difficult to wage an effective struggle because personnel are discharged at the end of their two-year compulsory service, just as they are becoming familiar with the region and the methods used in the struggle against terrorists." *Hurriyet* reported that in addition to the Public Security Army Corps, the existing "special team force" would be increased from 3,000 to 10,000 men, making a total of 35,000 men available to fight terrorists.

Martial law was in effect in four southeastern provinces--Siirt, Mardin, Hakkari and Diyarbakir--until July 19, 1987, when it was lifted and replaced by a state of emergency. A state of emergency still exists in four other eastern provinces as well: Bingol, Elazig, Tunceli and Van. In July the government appointed a regional governor for those eight provinces, with extra authority to combat the separatist insurgents, including command of the regional security forces and full authority to evacuate villages or rural settlements temporarily or permanently for security purposes. The state of emergency has been described as "civilian martial law;" its implementation was described in a statement issued by the regional governor:

> All citizens and visitors must carry identity cards; mukhtars [village headmen] will report suspicious aliens to the nearest security officials. Permits must be obtained from the provincial governors for rallies or demonstrations within the legal deadline. The bans previously imposed by the martial law command and the state of emergency governors on various publications remain in force. The production, possession, or transportation of explosives and inflammable material is subject to permit. Public organizations which have special protection and security systems are responsible for adopting and implementing their own security measures. A 24-hour telephone service will be available to citizens for their queries on the implementation of the state of emergency and for the supply of information on suspects. Those who violate these regulations will be prosecuted in accordance with the law. *Ankara Domestic Service*, July 19, 1987.

The Village Guards

In order to protect villages in the southeast from terrorist actions, the Turkish government has created "village guards"--local peasants who are paid monthly stipends and provided with arms. The village guards act as another military force in addition to the gendarmerie, army commandos and police. Each village has at least two or three village guards; on March 30, 1987, *Newsweek* estimated the total number of village guards at 6,000.

The government issues rifles to village guards; the use of these firearms is not tightly controlled. Regulations for village guards provide that a village guard:

- Can use his firearm against people who attack him or endanger his life;

107

- While doing his job, if he sees the life or honor of a person from the community endangered, and can't find any other means to save the person, he can use his firearm;
- If he sees a perpetrator in the act of murder or wants to apprehend a related person, he can use his firearm if that person resists;
- If a murderer who was apprehended escapes and does not obey an order to stop, and if there is no other way to catch him, he can use his firearm;
- During hot pursuit, if a man comes out of a banned location and does not obey an order to stop, the village guard can use his firearm;
- Village guards who are surprised by bandits may use their guns within the limits of the law, as do the gendarmerie;
- A village guard who uses his gun in other situations than those described above will be punished. A village guard must take care to apprehend a person to the extent possible by wounding but not killing, if he has to use his gun.

According to the *Ankara Domestic Service* of July 15, 1987, the Council of Ministers has ruled that village guards can carry personal weapons as well as official arms throughout their tours of duty.

The qualifications for the village guard post are minimal: guards must be between 22 and 60 years old, have no criminal record, be of good character and free of bad habits like drunkenness or causing fights.

The amount paid the village guards--54,900 Turkish lira, or about $67 a month--is a significant amount of money in a country where the per capita income has been estimated by various sources as from $1,250 to $3,000 a year. Usually the village headman is appointed as village guard; if he doesn't want the job, he can decide who will get it.

The village guard program has been sharply criticized by opposition politicians, press and people who live in the southeast. On April 19, 1987, *Cumhuriyet* quoted Erdal Inonu, Chairman of the SHP, who called on the government to dissolve the village guard institution, which he said caused strife among tribes in the east and kindled blood feuds. "Giving arms to such uneducated persons in order to provide the functions of the state which ought to be performed by the security forces of the state causes a multitude of incidents," he said. According to *Cumhuriyet*, Feb. 25, 1987, the Social Democratic People's Party, the Correct Way Party and the Democratic Left Party have all agreed that the system is not working and is exerting a negative effect.

Kenan Nehrozoglu, a member of Parliament from Mardin, is unhappy with the village guards. "They are a problem to the villagers; with their guns, rifles and pistols, they use force against their enemies in the villages. Tribal loyalties continue to play a part in the region, and the arming of one side of a blood feud can only lead to trouble. The security forces should protect the villages, not untrained village guards."

Nokta reported on April 26, 1987, that some village guards have been convicted of kidnapping women, arson and raiding homes. One villager told a *Nokta* reporter, "We no longer have peace, since these village guards were issued weapons. We are squeezed between the village guards and the PKK. We have to get along with the village guards. When they come to us we tell them, 'you are the greatest.' What would you do if you were in our shoes?"

A journalist in Mardin said:

> The village guards are a real problem--they put pressure on peasants to give them food, meat and chickens. And the government gives rifles to one side in a continuing struggle-- the other side is helpless and suffers. The state is not powerless--why does it give guns to one group and not others? I think the state wants to create a split in the villages... The state and the army have lost credibility by taking such exaggerated measures as arming village guards. We personally don't want people to lose confidence in the state and in the army.

Some villagers pressed into service by the military as village guards are not happy about their position. Osman Ildiz, a resident of Sirnak, told the *Associated Press*, February 26, 1987: "Local guards armed by the military are natural targets for the guerrillas. We prefer not to be armed and to be safe, but we cannot turn down the military."

In spite of the problems caused by the use of village guards and the resulting criticism, an announcement by Police Chief Saffet Arikan Beduk reported in the *Turkish Daily News*, June 25, 1987, indicated that the number of village guards in the eastern region may be increased.

Abuse of the Civilian Population

The government's efforts to subdue the terrorists have extended to the civilian population. Over and over we heard stories of the abuse of peasants by gendarmes, army, police and village guards. Often these involved incidents in which the military were searching for suspected terrorists; even more frequent were tales of abuse by the military of peasants whom they suspected of providing food for terrorists.

According to *Info-Turk*, September 1986, a group of SHP deputies who visited the Southeast in September 1986 reported at a press conference held on their return:

- Intimidation and fear is attaining such a level that the citizens, fearing that they will be harassed by the security forces for what they say, refuse to speak, even with the deputies they themselves elected.
- The militia, charged by the government with preventing Kurdish militants from entering the villages, abuse their power. Even people who have nothing to do with the Kurdish resistance are killed or threatened by this militia
- Since the government promised a reward of 2.5 million Turkish lira for information leading to identification of a suspect, there has been a sharp increase in the number of denunciations, some of which have no basis. In an area where the average income is barely 250,000 TL ($300), such a high sum incites citizens to inform on others.
- Kurdish citizens who don't know the Turkish language are submitted to arbitrary pressure and are constantly humiliated and maltreated.
- Underdevelopment in the region continues as before, and the state exists there only as a coercive force. Consequently, the confrontation between the population and the army is taking on alarming scale.

These conclusions were supported by Amnesty International in its June 15, 1987, report, "Continuing Violations of Human Rights in Turkey:"

For some time Amnesty International has received reports of widespread ill-treatment and torture carried out by government security forces in the East and South-East of Turkey connected with armed clashes between guerrilla groups and the security forces. Large numbers of the local civilian population have been detained and interrogated, and in many cases allegedly tortured ... Since the area is still under martial law, it has been very difficult for Amnesty International to obtain detailed information on specific cases.

On February 12, 1986, *Cumhuriyet* printed an interview with SHP Member of Parliament, Cuneyt Canver, who said:

East and southeast Anatolia have been transformed into a large penal camp. Everyone is afraid of everyone else. The people cannot speak, even criticize. When the villagers, out of fear, give the terrorists food ... the security forces come later ... and call the villagers to account for such actions.

Press reports have described the dilemma faced by Kurds in eastern Turkey: the Associated Press, February 26, 1987, quoted Yusuf Acu, the headman of Toptepe Village in Sirnak, a few miles from the Iraqi border: "We either offer the guerrillas food and face military persecution or deny them any help and get killed.... All we want is a better life."

In Ankara Kenan Nehrozoglu, a Member of Parliament from Mardin, told us there had been many complaints from Mardin villages about the military. In December in the Derik area, villages were surrounded by security forces; the villagers were not permitted to leave--this meant they could not plant the seeds that had to be planted in December. Nehrozoglu visited the area with newspaper reporters, who wrote stories on the situation; the military were taken from the village the next day.

Mr. Nehrozoglu also told us about an incident in Pinarbasi village in Mardin, in which security forces detained about 25 members of the family of a man being sought as a terrorist; the family was detained for more than 23 days at a gendarmarie station--they were told that they would be held there until the missing man turned himself in. When that didn't work, the gendarmerie told

111

the family that the father of the suspected terrorist and 15 other family members would have to leave the village with all their household goods. Hearing of the incident, Nehrozoglu went to the village; he told us: "All the family were crying, and the father said, 'It's my son's fault--I don't like him--why doesn't the government catch him?'" After Nehrozoglu intervened the captain of the gendarmerie station released the family.

Mr. Nehrozoglu said:

My concern is for the ordinary villagers. The government thinks everyone is a terrorist. The government's business is to catch terrorists--people in the villages don't support the terrorists, but if the terrorists come with guns, they are forced to give them food. Then the government goes after the villagers.

The last major incident like this happened in Gercus, in Mardin at the end of April or the beginning of May. Six villages were involved: Aricakoyu, Cukuryurt, Kocak, Yassica, and Guzel Oz. The security forces took all the people from these villages--ages 7 to 70, women and men. There were 45 to 60 people from each village-- they were taken to Ulas, where they were beaten and given electric shock; they were kept in a school building for two or three days and then let go. I went there eight or nine days later; lots of people had been injured, but were afraid to make complaints to officials. I could only persuade six people to complain. I took them to the prosecutor, who sent them to a doctor, who said they would not be able to work for another four to seven days. [Mr. Nehrozoglu gave us copies of the doctor's reports on all six.] The major in charge of the gendarmes is Aytakin Icmez, a commander who travels from place to place.

In May Besir Temiz, an old man with no gun, was sitting under some trees. The same commander, Major Icmez, saw him though binoculars and ordered his men to pick him up. When Temiz saw the soldiers coming, he ran away; sergeants shot and killed him. Later they said they were sorry, it had been a mistake. A week ago I saw the old man's family and filed a complaint against Icmez. The Gercus prosecutor rejected it and sent it to the military court in Diyarbakir. Nothing has happened yet.

We went to Mardin, a handsome city of 45,000 on a hill overlooking the Syrian border about an hour and a half by car from Diyarbakir. It is the major city in the province of Mardin; the province has a population of about 600,000.

In the local headquarters of the SHP we met with six men, officials and members of the SHP, and later, briefly, with the police chief. The SHP people confirmed Mr. Nehrozoglu's account of the events in Gercus concerning the rounding up, torture and detention of villagers from six villages. The case is now under investigation by the Gercus prosecutor. They told us it would be impossible to take us there; if villagers talked to us they would most likely be in serious trouble with the military. One man said there was little torture in Mardin province now, except for Gercus; he blamed the situation in Gercus on Major Aytakin Icmez, who is still in charge there.

The Mardin SHP people gave us more details on the death of Besir Temiz, who they said was mentally ill. Temiz, they said, had actually not run away when the soldiers approached him; the bullets had hit him in the front--in the lower chest and stomach. The prosecutor has started an investigation, but Temiz's relatives don't want to file a complaint--they are afraid of the officials.

A Mardin lawyer told us of another incident that had taken place in Nusaybin, a town of Mardin, a year earlier. A young man, Ibrahim Polat, on leave from military service, was picking grapes with his wife and mother when an armed struggle started between the PKK and the army. The PKK guerrillas ran away, and an officer asked Polat where they had gone. Polat said he didn't know, that he was a soldier too. The soldier, Sergeant Haydar Colakci, became angry and said, "Are you brave enough to answer me back?" and began kicking him. Polat was then taken away; his battered body was returned to his family the next day. Sergeant Colakci is still in charge of a gendarmerie unit.

The same lawyer said:

They are actually killing people who are poor and powerless, so the rest of the people will live in fear.... Minister of the Interior Akbulut was told about it, but said "it was only one man--don't make an issue of it."... Actually things are getting better, with the help of European public opinion--except in Gercus. But a feeling of instability and insecurity prevails. People are in the middle between the terrorists and the state. The gendarmes are young soldiers, 20 years old, who are told that behind every tree and rock is a terrorist. They are ready to attack anyone they meet. If anything happens to a friend in a confrontation with a terrorist, the soldier starts attacking people. On the other hand are the terrorists who come with guns asking for food. The people have no guns--what can they do?

Two days after our visit to Mardin we drove to Tunceli, a city of 19,000, about a four-hour drive north of Diyarbakir. Tunceli has long been a troubled area; the population of Tunceli province has fallen from 200,000 in 1975 to 162,000 in 1985, during a time when the population of Turkey has been climbing rapidly. According to the mayor of Tunceli people have left the area for two reasons:

... political pressure and economic needs. We have a lot of unemployed people. The province is poor--it is hungry for services. Our literacy rate is 93 percent, compared with 70 percent for Turkey as a whole; our people value education because this is a mountainous area, and it's very hard to support yourself on the land. So people see that the only way out is to be educated.

The military presence in Tunceli is palpable--uniforms are everywhere. Tunceli residents told us that a permanent brigade of 2,000 gendarmes is stationed there, as well as a commando troup of 300. Four or five helicopters are based near the town; one flew back and forth overhead the day we were there. We were told that three or four days before our visit jets had flown over and bombed mountainous areas nearby where terrorists were thought to be hiding.

"There is no privacy in Tunceli," a lawyer in Tunceli told us. "People are not safe in their own homes. Police and gendarmes go into any house or office any time they want. Most of the population are peasants; the police and gendarmes go to their homes at night and take them away--without any legal basis or legal documents." He also described a recent incident in Hozat, a nearby village:

114

A military operation was going on in Hozat; soldiers went to some peasants and forced them to act as guides to help find the terrorists. The soldiers found some terrorists and an armed struggle ensued. One of the terrorists, a girl, held up her hands to surrender; she was shot and killed by soldiers. Because the guides had witnessed the killing, soldiers shot at both of them-- one was killed, the other managed to run away. The name of the guide who was killed was Muslim Yagmur, who was 21 or 22. The other guide was his cousin, Ozgur Yagmur, about the same age. The terrorist who was killed was also from Hozat. This happened in May, maybe on the 20th. We invited the press to look into what happened; reporters came and went to Hozat, along with Fikri Saglar and Cuneyt Canver of the SHP, but the story never appeared in the papers.

One of the other men related an incident that also took place in May 1987:

In the village of Sarisaltik in Hozat, there was a fight between the gendarmes and some "runaways." Three soldiers were killed. The other soldiers were so vengeful that they surrounded the area. An hour later, they accused a 15-year-old girl and a 6-year-old boy who were tending their cows of helping the terrorists. Then they shot them; the girl was killed-- the boy is still in Diyarbakir Hospital. People in the village saw the whole thing. Nothing has happened to the soldiers.

In another incident on May 1, 1987, five girls were getting water at the village fountain in Sutlece; gendarmes opened fire--two were injured, the others ran away. The only reason given for the shooting was that the gendarmes thought the five had come together to celebrate May 1st. This incident was reported in the press.

A Tunceli lawyer described another cruel episode:

In the fall of 1986 soldiers were searching a village called Ors, in Muzgir. The owner of one house, an old man, told the officers: "You can search my house, all except one room where my daughter- in-law is giving birth." The officers kicked the door down anyway, with the old man resisting, and found the daughter-in-law giving birth. To punish the old man for resist-

115

ing, the soldiers tied his hands with rope and pulled him along with a jeep, driving slowly. The old man would stumble and fall down, then get up and be pulled along. The jeep came to another village; a higher ranking officer asked, "What's going on?" He told the officer in charge that he was wrong to have done it, but he didn't want the soldiers to lose face, so he told the old man that if he would kiss the hand of one of the soldiers (a mark of great respect in Turkey) he would be released. The soldier, upset at the prospect of an old man kissing his hand, began to cry. This incident was seen by several villagers.

Other incidents have been reported in the press and by Amnesty International:

- On March 3, 1987 *Cumhuriyet* reported that villagers in Kutlubey and Doganli villages in Nusaybin province had been harassed and tortured by the gendarmerie. After the incident in Doganli village, a report issued by the Health Office on February 20, 1987, stated that violence had been inflicted on Necmi Yildiz.
- Amnesty International in its June 15, 1987, report, "Continuing Human Rights Violations in Turkey," stated: "On 20 February 1987 the inhabitants of Demirisik village, near Kilis on the Syrian border, were reportedly told to gather in the centre of the village and parade to military orders. On refusal, the village headman Aziz Yusuf Ugurlu was beaten on his hands and another person was beaten on his head. On 5 March Mehmet Ugurlu, aged 36, Fayet Tatar, aged 45, and Mehmet Ugurlu, aged 24, from the same village were taken to the local gendarmerie station. Allegedly they were held for five days and were beaten with fists on their faces and with truncheons on their backs. After their release Mehmet Ugurlu and Fayet Tatar were medically examined and received a report from the Health Office stating that both had traumatic bruises on their thighs at the back of the left gluteal area."

Forced Migration

In recent months the Turkish press has carried many accounts suggesting that the government has undertaken, or is about to undertake, forcible relocation of peasants in villages both in the border areas in the southeast and in Tunceli. This would not be the first time such drastic steps have been taken:

in 1938 the government forcibly relocated tens of thousands of villagers from Tunceli, then known by its Kurdish name--Dersim. Refugees from the area report that thousands of Kurds were killed at that time; one told us that his father was the only survivor in a village of 42 homes. After a government amnesty in the 1950's many Kurds from Tunceli returned to their homes. But now the process seems to be beginning again.

International humanitarian law--the human rights component of the laws of war--prescribes protections for civilian populations in armed conflicts. Article 17 of Protocol II of the 1949 Geneva Conventions states:

> The displacement of the civilian population shall not be ordered for reasons related to the conflict unless the security of the civilians involved or imperative military reasons so demand. Should such displacements have to be carried out, all possible measures shall be taken in order that the civilian population may be received under satisfactory conditions of shelter, hygiene, health, safety and nutrition.

The actions of Turkish security forces, commandos, and other military personnel toward the peasants in Tunceli raise questions about Turkey's compliance with accepted norms of treatment of civilians in armed conflict situations.

The March 14-21, 1987, issue of the magazine *2000'e Dogru* contains an article about mass evacuations in Tunceli province in 1985.

The article reported that in August 1985 30 families including 270 people from Ormanyolu village in Hozat were forced out of their village. In July 1985 Major Naim Kurt, commander of an 8th Army battalion, raided the village with his soldiers. Everyone was gathered in the square and made to kneel. He said, "I give you three options: either become informers, or take to the mountains and become terrorists, or evacuate the village. You have twenty days." As a result of this and other pressure, beatings and torture, 15 families went to Akhisar and five to Salihli in Manisa, three to Ortaklar in Aydin, one to Derince in Izmir, four to Mersin and two to Elazig; all are now living in poverty.

According to the article, the gendarmerie demolished the houses and cut down thousands of birches and fruit trees. The villagers petitioned the Min-

117

istries of Public Works, Finance and Customs, Interior, Agriculture, Forestry and Village Affairs and the Tunceli governor's office, and presented copies of their deeds to the lands. They were then told that they could not claim any rights because they had left voluntarily. The peasants left behind their lands and animals; they were not compensated, given houses, jobs or any assistance.

Recently the government announced plans to deport 50,000 Tunceli villagers to the western provinces of Antalya, Mersin, Mugla and Izmir, where they would be provided with lands to be opened to agriculture. When opposition parties protested, the government denied that any order for collective migration had been given. Interior Minister Akbulut, however, acknowledged the policy by announcing that the migration from Tunceli and vicinity was not related to security or separatist forces. And State Minister Ahmet Karaevli said that hamlets in the east and southeast would no longer be provided with water or electricity so that they would be encouraged to move to larger units of settlement. In addition, the Expertise Commission studying the issue was said by *Cumhuriyet* in February 1987 to have included 3,192 villages on a list of villages to be moved. The relocation of villages is often explained as being part of a major reforestation project.

Ankara Anatolia, however, on May 4, 1987, reported government plans to move villages using the fight against terrorism as the motive:

> Villages and settlements spread out in Turkey's southeastern province of Tunceli will be united for protection against terrorism in the region as well as for better servicing by the state, official sources reported today.
>
> ... Tunceli's Governor Cengiz Bulut said the relevant project, approved by the Prime Ministry, will be implemented by the Ministry of Agriculture, Forestry and Village Affairs.
> Governor Bulut explained that separatist terrorists benefitted from the scattered situation of the settlement's units for their acts of violence.
>
> "There are over three thousand settlement units in the province of Tunceli, the population of which is 152,000. Some of the units comprise a few houses one kilometer apart. It is

118

difficult to take proper civil service to them all," Governor Bulut said.

The implementation will begin next year, the governor added.

In an interview in June 1987, Unal Marasli, the director of the Office of Research in the Foreign Ministry, told us that there was no forced migration from Tunceli or from anywhere else. He said that the government was planning to relocate people from forest areas in western Turkey as well, and not just from Tunceli, and that the relocation was voluntary. According to Mr. Marasli:

> The goal is to relocate people to better areas, to move people from poor villages to where there are better economic opportunities. It is not compulsory, and no one has been moved yet. A questionnaire was sent by the Ministry of Agriculture, Forestry and Village Affairs to 91,000 people in Tunceli; 78,000 people said they wanted to move. Villagers who said no or didn't take part will stay where they are. The villagers who leave will be sent to Antalya, Mersin, Izmir and Mugla in southwestern Turkey. The government will give them lands and credits, and will provide water, electricity, roads, schools and medical services. It is very expensive, and is a long-term project--it will be spread over some years, not two or three; it's only in the preliminary stages now.

In Tunceli we learned that two villages in Hozat had already been emptied--Yenibas and Ormanyolu. The peasants had gone to Denizli and Manisa, and their houses had been torn down. People had been told that the move was for forestry reasons, but the local leaders with whom we spoke believed that the real purpose was to assimilate the Kurds--to end their separate cultural existence. They described how, at the end of December 1986 every peasant had received a declaration from the Ministry of Agriculture, Foresty and Village Affairs saying that people would be taken "voluntarily" to Mersin, Antalya, Mugla and Izmir, and that their "voluntary declarations" would be collected. (See Appendix 8.) There were no questions on the declaration; it was simply a legal document telling the peasants they must leave.

119

Member of Parliament Elgin, from Icel, told a *Yeni Gundem* reporter that eleven villages in the province of Tunceli had been evacuated. One of the inhabitants, Mr. Caytasi, cried when he described his house being completely flattened to prevent him from returning. Mr. Elgin said that inhabitants were forced to sign statements saying they were "running away from terrorists." Peasants from the village of Yenibas were beaten when they refused to leave; eventually they were forced to go.

In Tunceli we were told what had happened in the village of Casitli in Hozat in 1986:

> The gendarmes went to the village at sunrise and gathered the whole population in the center of the village--women and children as well. They were made to lie face down in the sun on the ground all day long--no trees, no shade--until sunset. The gendarmes shouted at them all day long, "You are Kurdish. You must leave this place. Because you continue to stay, the PKK are here. If you were not here, the PKK would not be able to live in the mountains--you give them food."

A young teacher in Tunceli said: "People are told they will be moved to good places, with good land, but they are taken to places where there are no services--no road, water, or electricity. The state says, 'you are used to it, so live here.' And local people see them as monsters, because they don't speak the same language."

An elderly man described villagers as "so upset by the beatings and constant humiliation and threats that they gave up, sold their cows and possessions cheaply, hired trucks and left." A Tunceli lawyer described the pressure that is forcing the local people to leave:

> In Tunceli there is no right to live. Gendarmes go to your house at night and disturb you--they disturb you at your work, while you are feeding the cows, everywhere. People are obliged to leave-- they have to sign the papers. A peasant says, "I will die or I will go." When he leaves, he is made to tear down his house. So a person has two options: die or tear down his house and go. This is not a new policy--more than 15 villages have been forced to leave over the past five years. This

new document is only the legal framework for doing what the government had already done.

We were given the names of twenty villages for which the government has decided it will never provide services--roads, electricity, water, health facilities and schools; local people call them "snuffed out villages." There is no future for the people who live there; they will be forced to leave. In Hozat, the villages are: Karacauus, Esenevler, Kurukaymak, Koru, Kavuktepe, Kockozluca; in Mazgit in the Kirandere region, the villages are: Oymadag, Kushane, Otlukaya, Orenici, Dallibel, Atacinar, Alhan, Dayilar, Ibimahut, Sarikoc, Gulec, Koyukusagi, Dedebag and Akdoven.

Three Kurdish Refugees

In a bare room in the basement of a community center in a Canadian city in April 1987 we interviewed three Kurdish refugees who had recently fled to Canada from Turkey. Because they were afraid of repercussions against relatives still in Turkey, they asked us not to use their real names and adopted pseudonyms for the interviews.

Ali Asker

Ali Asker is a tall square-jawed young man of 28 with curly black hair, heavy eyebrows and a thick mustache. He was dressed in blue jeans and a blue checked shirt. Mr. Asker comes from Adiyaman in southeastern Turkey, west of Diyarbakir. His family--his wife and two children, his father and other relatives--are still in Adiyaman. His wife's uncle's sons are members of the PKK (Kurdish Workers' Party) for whom Turkey has asked the death penalty.

Mr. Asker, a farmer and peasant, left because of increasing oppression in Turkey. He finished elementary school in a small village in 1971. In order to send him to middle school, his parents had to take him to a larger town, Adiyaman. At first the authorities refused to register him because his father's first name was Kurdish. He was finally permitted to register; his own first name is not Kurdish.

121

Although more than half the students were Kurds, the teachers taught only in Turkish. Mr. Asker had trouble speaking proper Turkish and the other children laughed at him; he was upset, and wondered why he could not learn in Kurdish, his mother tongue. Because of his language problems, he left school and went back to his village (he did not want to tell us the name of the village). He then studied at home and passed a middle school examination. In 1977 he started high school in Adiyaman.

Memet Erdem, now the mayor of Adiyaman, was then the assistant director of the high school. One day in 1977 or 1978, when Mr. Asker was 18 years old, he found Mr. Erdem standing in the doorway of his school with some Neo-Fascists, followers of Alparslan Turkes. One of them hit Mr. Asker with chains, and said, "Can't you read what it says in the entrance?" Mr. Asker then saw a handprinted sign, just posted, that said, "Kurds and Alevis cannot enter this school." Mr. Asker and his friends were not allowed in. (The Alevis are a Shiite Moslem sect whose religious practices are different from those of the Sunnis. Some Alevis are Turks, some are Kurds; the number of Alevis in Turkey has been estimated at up to 15 million. Alevis are traditionally more liberal in their religious beliefs than Sunni Moslems.)

After that Mr. Asker stopped trying to go to school. He became increasingly sympathetic toward Kurdish national feelings and the struggle of the Kurdish people to maintain their identity.

In 1978 open conflict broke out between the Alevis and the Sunnis in Maras. Mr. Asker believes that as many as 2,000 may have died-- some Alevis, some Sunnis. He believes that the government was trying to increase conflict between the Alevis and the Sunnis in Maras, Adiyaman and Malatya. This also strengthened his sense of Kurdish identity.

In 1979 Mr. Asker went into the army to do his required military service; he was stationed at a gendarmerie station in

Karakocan, near Bingol. Although the town was Kurdish, he was not allowed to speak Kurdish.

In 1980 at the time of the military coup, Mr. Asker was still in the army, known as a Kurd and an Alevi. One month before he was due to leave the military, his gun was taken from him and he was put under observation. He was then released and sent to Adiyaman. In Adiyaman he and his father were both detained by the police, who accused both of espionage, saying they were Kurds and sympathizers of the PKK. They were then taken to a school outside Adiyaman which after the coup had become a torture center. The building was surrounded by military forces.

After three days his father had someone turn his gun over to the authorities and was released. (Mr. Asker told us guns are commonly kept in that part of Turkey for self-defense or to kill animals.) Mr. Asker, however, was detained for four months amd tortured throughout. He told us that 50 people died of torture while he was detained--he knew this because people talked in the cells about people who had died under torture. With his own eyes he saw the bodies of two people-- a doctor and a shepherd--carried past his cell by guards who said, "If you spread your views, your future will be like these dead people's." He told us that recently a cemetery with many bodies was uncovered there, but that the government said the bodies are centuries old and refused to permit an investigation.

Mr. Asker was tortured by "Palestine hanging," electric shocks and "train torture," in which bags of sand were pressed against both sides of his head while he was blindfolded. He was tortured once a week, sometimes on a Monday, sometimes on a Friday. Some people were tortured every day. He was tortured by teams of police--he did not know their names or where they came from. Three to six worked on him at a time; some tortured him, some rested. He was released in March 1981 and told to leave the province. No charges were ever filed against him.

123

After that Mr Asker went to Istanbul, where he sold melons on the street from a cart. Later in 1981 he went back to Adiyaman because he had a girlfriend in the village; the authorities didn't know that he had come back.

In April 1982 Mehmet Bozat, a government reporter, was killed by the PKK. This was a shock to government officials, who thought the PKK was no longer active in that area. They picked up everyone who had been tortured, including Mr. Asker. This time he was held for 8 months, first in Adiyaman, then in Diyarbakir and finally in Sanliurfa Prison. He was tortured irregularly, by the same methods. They tortured him to try to get information from him and to destroy his belief in the Kurdish nation. He showed us scars that remain from this period of torture: a 3- or 4-inch square light brown patch on the skin of his back above his waist which came from being burned with something (he was blindfolded at the time), and smaller scars on his right leg from cigarette burns.

Police accused Mr. Asker of being a PKK sympathizer, but no charges were filed against him. There were no legal proceedings, and he never saw a lawyer. After eight months he was released and told not to talk about the torture or his political beliefs in the struggle of the Kurds. He was told that he would be killed if he did.

Between 1982 and 1986 he worked in Istanbul in the summer and Adiyaman in the winter.

In 1986 he was detained for the third time. At that time government pressure had increased on the villagers: they were not allowed to cut trees for firewood, or to use tree leaves for their animals, nor were they allowed to grow tobacco. Mr. Asker and his friends tried to mobilize people to help them to press the government to change those policies. This was not done by the PKK, but by local people. The effort was successful, and the villagers were permitted to use the trees and leaves. But in February 1986 the police picked up Mr. Asker for his part in mobilizing the people.

First Mr. Asker was taken to Adiyaman for 10 days and tortured there. Then he was transferred to Diyarbakir for 21 days, where he was held in a military prison and tortured by police forces. He described Diyarbakir prison as a huge building surrounded by walls. He was in cell no. 7 at Kolordu Seyrantepe. In his section there were 12 cells with one prisoner in each. Although they were not supposed to talk to each other, some good-hearted officers used to let them talk with friends in other cells. Mr. Asker's cell was so small he could not lie down or fully extend his legs; he could only stand up or sit. There was no toilet or water in the cell. There was no window, only a small hole for guards to look through. The cell was always dark; it was impossible to tell day from night, unless you could hear the voice of the Mullah praying.

Mr. Asker was tortured in a special torture room at Diyarbakir by the same techniques, including the Palestine hanger. His torturers threatened to kill him. This time he was also asked questions while attached to a lie detector. Mr. Asker says he told the truth, but was upset and his heart was pounding--his questioners told him the lie detector showed that he was lying. They cursed at him, and used bad language about his mother, father, wife and children, which upset him further. Then he would be taken back to the torture room and tortured again, using the Palestine hanger technique. One day he was tortured on six separate occasions.

After 21 days in Diyarbakir Prison Mr. Asker was taken to a court for the first time and appeared before a judge; he was accused of being a member of the PKK. He told the judge that he was not a member of the PKK or any other group, that he was just trying to relieve the pressures on the villagers. The judge ordered him released.

When he was released he found that the resistance to the military had increased; some soldiers were killed and the government was shocked and sent in commando groups. These troops spoke Kurdish and tried to build up hatred against the PKK. They stole money from a woman and killed a shepherd and blamed it on the PKK. Police picked up Mr.

Asker and told him he had two months to create an event that would make people hate the PKK. He realized then that he couldn't stay in Turkey any longer. He read in the newspaper that Canada accepted refugees and that he could find work there, so he went to Istanbul and a policeman helped him get a passport which he used to come to Canada. Since leaving he has written to his wife and spoken with her on the telephone--both of them cried. She said the situation is bad, but could not say any more. Mr. Asker is now looking for work and living on $180 a month welfare from the Canadian government.

Aziz Kilic

Aziz Kilic is a soft-spoken, 33-year-old man of medium height; he has straight black hair and a mustache. He comes from Maras in central Turkey, west of Diyarbakir, where he was a peasant farmer; his wife is still there--they have no children. He arrived in Canada three or four months before our interview.

Mr. Kilic told us that he left Turkey for political reasons. He has been in prison twice; the first time was in April and May of 1981. After the military coup in 1980 he worked in the summer as a farmer, and was studying to be a teacher in the winter in Gaziantep, south of Maras, at a school formed by Kurdish students. At an anniversary of a 1978 action against Kurds the students held a protest demonstration; as a result the authorities closed the school and detained most of the students.

Mr. Kilic was held for 90 days at police headquarters where he was tortured. He was then taken before a judge, charged with being a progressive, and sent to a military prison, where he served two months. After his release he had to report to the police every day for four months, and then once a month. In 1986 he was picked up again in Maras, detained for 15 days and tortured again. At that time he was a member of a village council in a small town near Maras. The government sent the town a list of questions; they wanted to know how many people in the town were Alevis, Sunnis, Arabs and Kurds, and how

126

many mosques there were. Mr. Kilic and the others on the village council did not want to divide people by ethnic or religious groups, and refused to answer the questions properly. As a result, five people were picked up-- the mayor and all four council members; all of them had known they would be arrested if they didn't answer the questions.

They were taken to the gendarmerie station. Mr. Kilic was blindfolded, and given *falaka* on the soles of his feet. Afterwards, his feet were put into ice to get rid of the evidence of *falaka*. He and the others were beaten, not to elicit more information, but because they hadn't given the government the facts it wanted. They were held for two weeks, but tortured only for the first week--tortured for three days, not tortured for two days, then tortured again. The torture was carried out by soldiers, not by police. All the people in the building were soldiers, specially trained for torture. He thinks they were trained in Germany. After 15 days he was released. No charges were ever filed.

It was after that detention that Mr. Kilic decided he had to leave. He bought a passport, flew from Istanbul, and arrived in Canada at the end of December 1986. Since his arrival he has spoken with his wife, who tells him that the oppression is increasing. Soldiers have taken old people and children to the center of the village and have hit young children, boys and girls 11 and 12 years old. He says the soldiers hit the children because they hate Alevis and Kurds.

Remzi Akbas

Remzi Akbas is a slight, olive-skinned 26-year-old man with straight black hair and a neatly trimmed mustache. He came to Canada from Malatya in eastern Turkey west of Diyarbakir toward the end of 1986 as a political refugee. He had been a peasant farmer.

At first Mr. Akbas was reluctant to tell us why he had left Turkey, as he was afraid his words would be used against his relatives in Turkey. After we told him that his real name would

127

not be used, nor details that would identify him, he agreed to talk freely.

Mr. Akbas spent two years in prison, from 1982 to 1984. He had been a university student; there had been a fight between Turks and Kurds. He was taken to the police station where his group was accused of being separatists. He was sent to Mersin Prison, which he called an E-type prison, a special type of prison built after the 1980 coup. There are 6 or 7 prisons of this type, not all in Kurdistan. It is worse than other prisons; the people who built it said it was an American-type prison.

In prison he was forced to pray a certain way and to read Turkish nationalistic poems which were very offensive to him. He was forced to sing Turkish anthems every morning, and was beaten if he didn't sing loud enough. He was tortured using *falaka* and electric shock. Sometimes electric wires were attached to both thumbs, sometimes to one thumb and his penis. He was then asked for names of people active in Kurdish activities. If he didn't give a satisfactory answer, an electric shock was sent through his body, powerful enough to knock him to the floor. This happened to him 10 or 15 times in the first 90 days in prison. He was also hung from a hook in the ceiling; his arms were tied behind his back and he was suspended from the hook by ropes tied to his wrists [the Palestine hanger]. His feet were not touching the floor; his body twisted around and he would get dizzy. The longest time he spent like this was about 10 minutes. Doctors were always present when he was hung like this; the doctor would check the time and tell the torturer, "Enough time, bring him down." Then the doctor would check his joints, and give him a physical examination. Every day after the torture, a doctor would check those who had been tortured to see if there was any permanent damage, or if it was all right to torture them in the future. The doctor would say, "You are good enough to be tortured again." Mr. Akbas did not know the names of any of the doctors; he knew they were doctors only because of the way they acted and the fact that they wore stethoscopes around their necks.

128

After being tortured Mr. Akbas would be made to stand in freezing water; he couldn't sit--if he sat down a guard would beat him.

Throughout the 90 days Mr. Akbas was always blindfolded except when he ate, when he was allowed to push the blindfold up so that he could see his food. He was not allowed to move in his cell, to lie down, or to speak.

After the first 90 days he was moved to a place where there were 60 people in one room. There were 11 bunk beds which were moved together for all the men to sleep on. They were taken from the room only once a day for the Turkish national anthem. There was no exercise. The food was normal military food; they used wooden spoons and forks. The toilet was in a separate room. They were allowed to wash once in 15 days; in the summer they were allowed showers but not in the winter. They wore prison clothes which they washed themselves when allowed. Once in 15 days it was possible to have visitors, but the visitors were far away, and they could see them only for a few seconds, enough to wave and say, "I'm all right, don't worry."

After two years he was taken before a judge in a military court and charged with making propaganda for Kurdistan. His hands were tied; he had no lawyer. The judge read the charges. He was acquitted, as there was no proof of the charges against him.

After his release, Mr. Akbas decided he had to leave. He got passports for himself and his wife with no difficulty; he bought them through friends and flew from Istanbul to Canada.
Mr. Akbas told us that, as bad as the electric shock and other tortures were, he felt it was worse to be forced to sing Turkish songs. He felt the authorities were forcing him to feel separate from society--that he was accused of being a Kurd, and not part of the whole country.

He believes that what is happening to the Kurds is tragic--and it is tragic that the world doesn't know about it. "People are

129

concerned with species of animals and birds, but no one is concerned about us. We are about 16 million people, but we have no right to have schools in our own language, and no right to express our own identity. In this century, our people are living in primitive conditions, with no electricity and no roads." He never belonged to a party in Turkey. He believes in human rights; he sees people as individuals, and does not want to separate them by race or religion.

VI. THE ROLE OF THE UNITED STATES AND WESTERN EUROPE

The United States and Turkey

In *Freedom and Fear*, the Helsinki Watch report of March 1986, we wrote:

> Turkey, a bulwark in the NATO system, is of great strategic importance to the West. Poised at the crossroads between Europe and the Middle East, it shares boundaries with Greece, Bulgaria, Iran, Iraq and Syria, as well as a sea and land border with the Soviet Union that runs some 1,000 linear miles. There are more than five thousand U.S. troops stationed in Turkey. U.S. intelligence agencies carry on electronic surveillance operations in Turkey, monitoring the Soviet Union, Iran and other strategic areas. Turkey maintains an army larger than that of West Germany or Great Britain and is fully aware of its importance to the West. Dr. Sukru Elekdag, Turkish Ambassador to the United States, recently stressed: "Turkey, one of 16 NATO countries, defends one third of the NATO frontier. This indicates dramatically the important role that we play."
>
> The United States government, deeply aware of Turkey's significance, maintains an important defense pact with Turkey. Turkey is the third largest recipient of U.S. military aid.... The Turkish government wants still more military aid in order to modernize its armed forces. It objects to the routine annual Congressional cut in the aid package. It objects to the 7-10 ratio by which military aid is targeted for Greece and Turkey....
>
> Turkey places great importance on its relations with the West. Financial aid is a large part of it, of course, but there is also the wish to be fully integrated into the Western alliance and not to be treated as a second-class partner. Turkish leaders,

following the direction established by Ataturk, are proud of
the fact that they are the only Moslem country that considers
itself part of Europe and the West.

For these reasons, it is humiliating for Turkish leaders to have
their country singled out as the only egregious human rights
offender in NATO. Their efforts to correct that impression-
-by suppression of the facts, by denial of the accusations, by
attempts to reform the system, and by negotiations with accusing countries--stem from their desire to be accepted fully in
the Alliance.

In 1987, Turkey became increasingly upset by the level of U.S. aid; for
fiscal year 1987 Congress authorized $493.3 million in military aid and $100 million in Economic Support Funds--a reduction of $135 million from the previous
year. For fiscal 1988 the administration has recommended $925 million; the
Senate and House foreign affairs committees recommended a cut to $569 mil-
lion. There has been no final decision as yet.

Turkey has also been angered by an attempt by the Senate Foreign
Relations Committee to link U.S. military aid to the Cyprus problem; the committee embargoed the use of U.S.-made weapons in Cyprus and demanded that
troop strength be reduced if U.S. aid is to continue.

Another very sensitive issue--perhaps the most sensitive of all--was a
resolution adopted by the House of Representatives' Post Office and Civil Service Committee that would proclaim April 24th "a national day of remembrance
of the Armenian genocide of 1915-1923." After much lobbying by Turkey and by
the U.S. State Department against the resolution, it was defeated on August 7,
1987, when the House of Representatives voted 201 to 189 not to debate the bill.

The Turkish government's unhappiness with these three issues led to
a postponement of President Evren's scheduled visit to Washington in late May
1987.

The Turkish government was also offended by the U.S. State
Department's 1986 *Country Report* on Turkey, which contains several
paragraphs on the Kurdish issue. According to *Cumhuriyet*, April 9, 1987, the

Foreign Ministry strongly expressed its dissatisfaction with the *Country Report* to the U.S. Embassy in Ankara.

In addition to adding some discussion of the Kurdish problem to its 1986 Country Report, the United States State Department in the past few years has become increasingly open in acknowledging the general human rights problems in Turkey. The State Department now pays greater attention to problems such as torture, imprisonment for crimes of thought, limitations on free expression and other human rights violations. During an official visit to Turkey in October 1986, Richard Schifter, Assistant Secretary of State for Human Rights and Humanitarian Affairs, met with private citizens involved in human rights activities in Turkey, including some members of the Turkish Peace Association whose trial was pending at the time. Ambassador Schifter's willingness to hear a diversity of views while in Turkey departs from the precedent set by his predecessor. Moreover, Ambassador Schifter refrained from making public statements during his visit, perhaps an indication of his recognition of the complexity of the situation in Turkey and his unwillingness to appear to be an apologist for the Turkish government's human rights policies.

At one time the State Department, attributing most of the torture in Turkey to police brutality caused by untrained police officers, was pressing for an amendment to Section 660 of the Foreign Assistance Act--the section that prohibits the training of foreign police forces by the United States. The suggestion was to permit the use of foreign assistance funds for the instruction of police personnel on citizens' rights and the creation of mechanisms to ensure the respect by policemen of these rights. Helsinki Watch has serious reservations about such a policy and its possible negative implications for the United States which might subsequently be blamed for any torture that continues. Recently the Department appears to have backed away from that position.

Ambassador Schifter and the U.S. Embassy in Ankara were extremely cooperative, supportive and helpful to us in planning and carrying out our recent visit to Turkey. Their attempts to persuade the Turkish government to change its mind about denying us meetings with high level officials, although unsuccessful, were much appreciated. The staff of the Embassy in Ankara was resourceful and helpful in the planning of our schedule.

Despite recent strains in U.S.-Turkey relations, the United States, because of its long history of friendship with and aid to Turkey, remains in a good position to encourage Prime Minister Ozal's administration to improve its human rights record. We hope that the United States will continue to increase its efforts in this direction.

Western Europe and Turkey

In 1982 five European nations--Denmark, France, the Netherlands, Norway and Sweden--filed a complaint with the European Commission of Human rights charging Turkey with:
- Violations of Articles 3, 5, 6, 9, 10 and 11 of the European Convention on Human Rights, relative respectively to prohibition of torture and inhuman or degrading punishments or treatments; individual's right to freedom and security; right to a fair trial before an independent and impartial tribunal; freedom of opinion, conscience and religion; freedom of expression; freedom of meeting and association.

The complaint and other actions by countries of Western Europe have been substantial forces in bringing about human rights improvements in Turkey. On December 7, 1985, however, a "friendly settlement" was reached between Turkey and the five nations, based on the Turkish government's promises to improve conditions in detention centers and prisons, to lift martial law from all provinces within 18 months, and to modify legislation concerning fundamental rights and freedoms and releases of people imprisoned for crimes of thought. Many believe that the "friendly settlement" was premature, based more on promises by the Turkish government than on specific actions.

On January 19, 1987, the European Commission of Human Rights closed the complaint file, acquitting Turkey of the charges. In a report issued on January 30, 1987, the Commission said that its decision was based on:
- the release of more than 31,000 convicted prisoners under the Reduction in Sentences Law;
- improved conditions in military detention centers and prospects for continued improvement in those centers;

- investigations into prison conditions carried out by the Parliamentary Committee;
- the Turkish government's determination to investigate allegations of torture and prosecute those responsible;
- the independence and impartiality of Turkish courts of law; and improvement in conditions in police detention centers.

It is unfortunate that this file was closed while torture and other human rights abuses continue in Turkey. It removes a source of pressure on the Turkish government and sends a misleading message to the rest of the world.

In April 1987 Turkey formally applied for full membership in the European Community, of which Turkey has been an associate member since 1963. Full membership would, of course, have important economic advantages for Turkey--greater trade, free circulation of workers throughout the Common Market--and the issue is considered very important by the Ozal government. Most commentators believe that the application process may take as long as ten or fifteen years, however, and that Turkey's admission is not guaranteed.

Turkey's eagerness to join the European Community presents Europeans with a new source of leverage with regard to Turkey's human rights practices. The government's decisions to hold a referendum on lifting the ban on former political leaders, to end martial law in the southeast and to allow the right of individual petition to the European Commission of Human Rights are all reflections of Turkey's continuing effort to solidify its position with the west and to gain full membership in the European community. Although resistance to Turkey's membership stems from economic as well as political factors, some member nations have raised Turkey's human rights practices as an obstacle to membership.

Objections to Turkey's admission as a full partner have been raised by many of the twelve current members. *The Wall Street Journal*, April 22, 1987, quoted Luxembourg's foreign minister, Jacques Poos, as "worried about Turkey's human rights record, why it hasn't yet returned to full democracy, its occupation of Northern Cyprus and its still not fully developed economy." British Foreign Secretary Sir Geoffrey Howe was quoted in the *Turkish Daily News*, April 14-20, 1987: "... human rights would be among the features taken into account in evaluating the application." According to *Cumhuriyet*, April 9,

1987, Foreign Minister Van Den Broek of Holland expressed reservations about Turkey's application: "The progress recorded in the democratization of Turkey cannot be overlooked, but that process can only be completed if further steps are taken. ... Your Western friends are waiting regarding this matter."

In June 1987, the European Parliament passed a resolution that called on Turkey to recognize the "genocide" against the Armenian people under the Ottoman Empire 70 years ago; not to deny the existence of the Kurds as a separate entity within the country; and to withdraw its troops from Cyprus. The resolution asked that these issues be considered before Turkey's application for full membership in the European Community is accepted. The Turkish government expressed outrage. According to *The Christian Science Monitor*, June 29, 1987, President Evren said: "It might be useful to review our ties with NATO in the light of recent developments." The European Parliament is a constituent body of the European Community (EC); it can advise the EC's Council of Ministers and Commission on legislation and policy.

The European Parliament's June 1987 resolution was the latest in a series of resolutions concerning human rights in Turkey. On December 11, 1986, the Parliament adopted a resolution citing findings of Amnesty International and Helsinki Watch on the widespread use of torture in prisons and in police stations and on the lack of fair trials in Turkey. In part, the resolution called for:

1. Continued progress toward the full restoration of parliamentary democracy in Turkey;

2. Action by the Turkish authorities to restore full human rights observance, notably as regards:

a) an amnesty for prisoners of conscience;
b) ending torture and inhuman prison conditions;
c) the right to a fair trial;
d) the discontinuance of the mass trials of the Turkish Peace Association, DISK and its affiliated unions, and various groups of intellectuals;
e) removing the restrictions on freedom of political activity, trade union rights and free expression of opinion;

f) abolition of the death penalty.

. . .

4. [The European Parliament] feels that the European Community is not yet justified in fully normalizing its relations with Turkey. . . .

VII. RECOMMENDATIONS

In *Freedom and Fear* (Helsinki Watch, March 1986), we made a number of recommendations to the Turkish government which we believed would lead to significant improvements in human rights in Turkey. Four of these recommendations have been accomplished.

First, on January 28, 1987, the Turkish government recognized the right of individual appeal to the European Commission of Human Rights. This is potentially a very important step; Turkish citizens should now be able to file individual complaints with the Commission about human rights violations in Turkey. Unfortunately the government qualified its recognition in a number of ways, and the matter has yet to be tested. (See *Legal Safeguards*)

Second, the government has permitted the establishment of a Human Rights Association which is now monitoring many of the human rights problems in Turkey.

Third, the government released from detention members of the Turkish Peace Association and DISK while their trials were in progress; many other prisoners of conscience, however, are still being detained, although the number is not certain.

Fourth, on September 6, 1987, the Turkish electorate voted by a narrow margin to rescind Provisional Article 4 of the Constitution, which banned former politicians from taking part in politics.

All four of these developments are important steps toward increasing human rights and democratic freedoms in Turkey. There are still many other steps that need to be taken.

We recommended in 1986, and recommend again today, that, with regard to eliminating torture, the Turkish government should:

- Admit to the fact that the problem of torture in Turkey continues routinely on a scale considerably more extensive than "isolated cases of police brutality;"

139

- Pass legislation guaranteeing the right of detainees to be represented by attorneys from the moment of detention and providing punishment for those who do not comply with this rule;
- The permissible period of detention before a detainee is brought before a judge and charged should be reduced in the case of both individual and collective crimes to a uniform 24 hours throughout Turkey;
- Require that police detention centers be investigated, by judges or other independent investigators, frequently, without notice, and without waiting for torture victims to initiate complaints;
- Establish a separate parliamentary committee to investigate police detention centers;
- Establish a single impartial body to which torture victims may bring complaints of torture;
- Eliminate any time restrictions on prosecuting charges of torture;
- Increase sentences for torturers;
- Provide periodic reports not only on the number of torturers sentenced but on the specific sentences that they received and where they are incarcerated;
- Provide medical and psychological treatment for torture victims, as well as financial compensation.

With regard to prison conditions, we recommended in 1986 and continue to recommend today that the Turkish government should:
- Take steps to implement as quickly as possible all recommendations contained in the report of the parliamentary committee on prison conditions issued in 1985;
- Encourage the parliamentary committee on prison conditions to continue its work by investigating all the as-yet-uninvestigated prisons in Turkey;
- Allow the International Committee of the Red Cross and other international organizations to visit detainees and prisoners in Turkish prisons and detention centers;
- Take steps to pass an immediate amnesty for all prisoners of conscience and to find humane ways to reintegrate other political prisoners into Turkish life;
- Release prisoners of conscience whose trials are in progress or whose sentences are on appeal but who are nevertheless being held in prison;

- Establish a special status for detainees so that they are not required to wear prison uniforms before being convicted;
- Provide open, comfortable surroundings for prison and detention center visits between prisoners and their families and lawyers;
- Forbid prison officials from punishing prisoners by denying them visiting privileges;
- Allow prisoners to receive food, clothing and books as gifts from outside;
- Pass legislation preventing the present inhuman and degrading methods of transferring prisoners from prison to prison and from prison to court or to hospital facilities.

With regard to free expression, we again recommend that the government:

- Cease all legal actions against the press and against writers and publishers that are based on the substance or means of circulation of their writings;
- Restore autonomy to the universities with regard to the selection of faculty and curriculums;
- Allow independent organizations, associations, professional institutions and trade unions to operate in Turkey and to be involved in politics;
- Restore the jobs of persons who were fired under martial law, including university professors, teachers and civil servants;
- Transfer to civilian courts cases presently being tried in martial law courts, except cases of military discipline against members of the armed forces.

Because many of these recommendations conflict with the 1982 Constitution and other legislation, we continue to recommend that Turkish authorities take steps to:

- Amend the Constitution so that legislation to accomplish the above recommendations may be passed;
- Amend the Turkish Penal Code so that it separates political acts of conscience from political crimes of violence and eliminates arbitrary and repressive articles such as Article 140 which makes it a crime to publish information abroad that is considered detrimental to Turkey's national interests;

141

- Eliminate other repressive legislation, such as Law No. 2969 which bars support of former politicians and political parties and which makes it a crime to criticize any actions taken by the martial law government from the takeover in September 1980 to the parliamentary elections in November 1983;
- Establish in the parliament an ombudsman system and/or a human rights committee to oversee and report on human rights violations.

In addition, as a result of our investigation into problems of the Kurdish minority, we recommend that the Turkish government:

- Acknowledge the existence of the Kurds and grant them the political and civil rights held by other Turks;
- End restrictions that deprive Kurds of their ethnic identity: permit use of the Kurdish language, music and dance and the celebration of Kurdish holidays; permit the use of Kurdish names; permit the Kurdish language to be used by prisoners, visitors and lawyers in prisons and detention centers;
- Permit the establishment of Kurdish associations and the publication of Kurdish books and periodicals;
- Establish a parliamentary commission to investigate the problems of the Kurdish minority and recommend steps to improve the situation;
- Abolish the village guard system;
- Take steps to protect the civilian population in the areas where guerrilla warfare is taking place;
- Punish appropriately abuse and humiliation of civilians by security or other military forces;
- End the harassment of Kurdish refugees abroad, for example by permitting Kurdish names to be given to children, and Kurdish to be listed, where indicated, as a person's mother tongue;
- End efforts to relocate civilians from troubled areas except in instances where their lives are endangered, and then only in accordance with Protocol II of the 1949 Geneva Conventions.

We remain concerned with gross abuses of human rights in Turkey, especially with regard to the use of torture. We deplore the continuation of repressive legislation in Turkey that provides no legal safeguards, even for those rights that Turkish citizens are now exercising.

As we said in 1986, these recommendations, although far from all-in-clusive, would, if implemented, go a long way toward improving the human rights situation in Turkey. The United States, to the greatest extent possible, should encourage the Turkish government to adopt them so that human rights observance in Turkey becomes a reality.

APPENDIX 1

Annex to letter JJ1939C
dated 29 January 1987
Tr./5 : Declaration Article 25

Declaration by the Government of Turkey
pursuant to Article 25 of the
Convention for the Protection of Human Rights
and fundamental Freedoms

The Government of Turkey, acting pursuant to Article 25 (1) of
the Convention for the Protection of Human Rights and Fundamental
Freedoms hereby declares to accept the competence of the European
Commission of Human Rights to receive petitions according to Article
25 of the Convention subject to the 'ollowing:

(i) the recognition of the right of petition extends only to
allegations concerning acts or emissions of public authorities in
Turkey performed within the boundaries of the territory to which the
Constitution of the Republic of Turkey is applicable ;

(ii) the circumstances and conditions under which Turkey, by virtue
of Article 15 of the Convention, derogates from her obligations under
the Convention in special circumstances must be interpreted, for the
purpose of the competence attributed to the Commission under this
declaration, in the light of Articles 119 to 122 of the Turkish
Constitution:

(iii) the competence attributed to the Commission under this
declaration shall not comprise matters regarding the legal status of
military personnel and in particular, the system of discipline in the
armed forces ;

(iv) for the purpose of the competence attributed to the Commission
under this declaration, the notion of "a democratic society" in
paragraphs 2 of Articles 8, 9, 10 and 11 of the Convention must be
understood in conformity with the principles laid down in the Turkish
Constitution and in particular its Preamble and its Article 13 ;

(v) for the purpose of the competence attributed to the Commission
under the present declaration, Articles 33, 52 and 135 of the
Constitution must be understood as being in conformity with Article 10
and 11 of the Convention.

This declaration extends to allegations made in respect of
facts, including judgments which are based on such facts which have
occurred subsequent to the date of deposit of the present declaration.
This declaration is valid for three years from the date of deposit
with the Secretary General of the Council of Europe.

145

APPENDIX 2

Human Rights Association
List of 149 Who Died in Detention

Officially said to have committed suicide (24):

Bekir Dağ, Celal Kıpırdamaz, Cumali Ay, Ahmet Karlangaç, Ahmet Hilmi Fevzioğlu, Abdurrahman Aksoy, İrfan Çelik, Satılmış Şahin Dokuyucu, Vedat Aldoğan, Veysel Yıldız, Abdullah Paksoylu, Ahmet Erdoğdu, Süleyman Cihan, Rafet Demir, Recep Estik, Hasan Hüseyin Duman, Mehmet Ceren, Mazlum Doğan, Ferhat Kurtay, Necmi Öner, Eşref Anyık, Mahmut Zengin, Suphi Çevirici, Hakkı Kocaoğlu.

Killed in torture at police headquarters, stations or prisons (97):

Ali Kılıç, Ayhan Alan, Ali Uygur, Ahmet Uzun, Ali Adil Yılmaz, Ali Küçük, Ahmet Atlan, Ali Çiçek, Ali Çakmak, Ali Özbey, Bedii Tan, Bahar Yıldız, Bozan Çimen, Bayram Kocabaş, Cafer Dağdoğan, Behçet Dinlerer, Bedri Sınak, Hulusi Dalak, Hasan Gazioğlu, Ercan Koca, Zeynel Abidin Ceylan, İbrahim Eski, Hasan Asker Özmen, Cabbar Demirok, Cuma Özaslan, Cennet Değirmenci, Ekrem Ekşi, Necmettin Büyükkaya, Mehmet Kazgan, Mustafa Yalçın, Niyazi Gündoğdu, Metin Sarpbulut, Mehmet Mutlu Çetin, Mustafa Hayrullahoğlu, Veysi Şimşek, Mustafa Taş, Osman Mehmet Önsoy, Hasan Hakkı Erdoğan, Akın Tanış, İbrahim Polat, Bahadır Dumanlı, Hakan Mermeroluk, Şeref Yazar, Hamdi Filizcan, Ali İnan, Mazlum Güder, Mustafa Işık, Behzat Ak, Coşkun Altan, Haydar Sönmez, Necip Kutlu, Şadan Gazeteci, Süleyman Ölmez, Şükrü Gedik, Sinan Karaçalı, Şadiye Yavuz, Yaşar Okçuoğlu, Hasan Kılıç, Hüseyin Çolak, Haydar Yağmur, Hasan Çelik, Haydar Öztürk, İbrahim Ulaş, İsmail Kıran, Kenan Küçük, Mehmet Cizreli, Munzur Geçzel, Nihat Arda, Mustafa Şahin, Aziz Ağaç, Osman Karaduman, Yılmaz Peköz, Sıddık Bilgin, Bedri Bilge, Alaettin Gülmüş, Kenan Kılıç, Cemal Kılıç, İsmet Karak, Ali Erek, İbiş Vural, Remzi Yalvaç, Abdülkadir Tapu, Asker Demir, Sait Şimşek, İlhan Erdost, Ataman İnce, Ali Sarıbağ, Aziz Özbay, Abdurrahman Geçen, Aziz Büyükertaç. Ensar Karahan, Oruç Korkmaz.
Fayrettin Eren, Nurettin Yedigöl, Maksut Tepeli, Gazal

146

Died from lack of medical care after torture (14):

Hasan Alemiioğlu, İsmet Baş, Adil Can, Abdullah Gürbudak, Mustafa Tepeii, Mustafa Tunç, Hüseyin Aydın, İsmet Taş, Zafer Müctebaoğlu, Şazuman Kansu, Turan Çağlar, Haluk Aydın, Bekir Çelenk, Fikri Sönmez.

Said to have been apprehended dead after battles with security forces (4):

Behzat Baykal, İsmail Cüneyt, Selma Aybal, Zeki Yumurtacı.

Died in hunger strikes protesting prison conditions and practices (10):

Mehmet Fatih Öktülmüş, Abdullah Meral, Hasan Telci, Haydar Başbağ, Akif Yılmaz, Kemal Pir, Mehmet Hayri Durmuş, Ali Çiçek, Orhan Keskin, Cemal Arat."

HRA Addendum to Report on Deaths in Detention

Name	Date	Location
Mehmet Metin Aksoy	1980	9th Army, Erzurum
Cemil Kirbayir	Sept 1980	Gole
Turan Saglam	Nov. 1980	Erzurum
Mehmet Karados	April 1981	Erzurum
Hasan	1985	Erzurum
Mahmut Kaya	1981	Kars, 1st Division
Sukru Gedik		Ogretmen
Ali Guven	1983	Izmir-NarliderKarakolu
Mehmet Andan	Aug. 27, 1986	Diyarbakir-Lice
Hidayet Akin	Feb. 12, 1987	Ankara Police Headqu'trs. Allegedly jumped from fifth floor
Yilmaz Demir		Diyarbakir
Vasif Ozaltin		Diyarbakir
Cemalettin Yalcin		Istanbul
Abdurraham Aktimur		Mardin-Masidag
Ihsan Cetintas		Erzurum
Zulfikar Bayram	1987	Diyarbakir
Orham Erdagli		Denizli-Kale
Sah Ismail Sat	1984	Kars
Ensar Karahan	1981	Artvin
Adnan Tuysuz	1987	Ceylanpinar

147

APPENDIX 3

SHP Secretary General Fikri Saglar's list of 253 political detainees who have either died during interrogation or disappeared since their arrest (as printed in *Info-Turk*, Nov. 1986.):

LIST OF THE DISAPPEARED

The secretary general of the Social-Democrat Populist Party (SHP) Fikri Saglar drew up a file comprising the names of 253 political detainees who have either died during their interrogation or disappeared since their arrest.

He said he would present this list to the National Assembly and demand precise explanations on the fate of these victims.

DEAD UNDER TORTURE

Fikri Saglar'ın dosyasında işkence nedeniyle ölen kişilerin adları şöyle sıralanıyor:

Zeynel Abidin Ceylan (Ankara) 26.9.1980, Şadan Gazeteci (İzmit) 26.9.1980, Hasan Asker Özmen (Ankara) 5.10.1980, Ekrem Ekşi (İstanbul) 13.10.1980, İlhan Erdost (Ankara) 7.11.1980, Hasan Kılıç (Elazığ) 30.12.1980, Ataman İnce (İstanbul) 25.10.1981, Ensar Karahan (Artvin) 1981, Haydar Sönmez (Elazığ) 6.3.1982, Vakkaş Devamlı (K.Maraş) 3.1982, Cennet Değirmenci (Gaziantep) 22.5.1982, Mustafa Hayrullahoğlu (İstanbul) 16.11.1982, Şahismail Şut (Kars) 14.12.1984.

Eyüp Akkurt (Gaziantep) 9.1980, Ömer Aktaş (Diyarbakır) 1.10.1980, Ahmet Karlangaç (İstanbul) 15.10.1980, Metin Aksoy (Ağrı) 24.10.1980, Cemil Kırbayır (Kars) 10.1980, Cengiz Aksakal (Artvin) 10.11.1980, Kenan Gürsoy (Diyarbakır) 3.12.1980, Fırcan Koca (Ankara) 14.12.1980, Cafer Dağdoğan (Adana) 16.12.1980, Sinan Karacah (Adana) 1.1981, Ömer Aydnğmış (İzmir) 12.2.1981, Hulusi Talak (Gaziantep) 13.2.1981, Bedrettin Sınak (Adana) 2.1981, Ahmet Demir (Diyarbakır) 2.1981, Nurettin Yedigöl (İstanbul) 10.4.1981, Hasan Ali Damar (Yahyalı/Kayseri) 12.5.1981, Sevim Akbaş (İstanbul) 18.5.1981, Mehmet Ceren (K.Maraş) 20.10.1981, Zafer Müçtehaşığlu (Ankara) 15.10.1981, Süleyman Aslan (Tokat) 20.11.1982, Feyzullah Bingöl (Muş) 25.11.1982, Ali Güven (İzmir) 28.7.1983, Enver Sabsn 12.11.1985, Hasan Hakkı Erdoğan (İstanbul) 18.9.1984, Sıddık Bilgin (Bingöl) 31.7.1985, Akın Tanış (İstanbul) 10.1985, Hamza İutan (Hakkâri) 8.11.1985, Recep Tuna (İstanbul) 27.1.1986, Hasan Çelik (Çorum) 12.2.1986, Ömer Çorak (Zonguldak) 5.7.1986, Yüksel Topdoğan (Ankara) 13.8.1986, Şükrü Baş (Malatya), Battal Evren, Ramazan Gören (Pötürge), Mazlum Güder (Elazığ) 3.1983, Haydar Yağmur (İstanbul).

DOUBTFUL "SUICIDES"

İrfan Çelik (İstanbul) 14.9.1980, Ali Çakmaklı (Adana) 25.9.1980, Rafet Demir (Bursa) 22.9.1980, Ali İnan (İstanbul) 28.9.1980, Ahmet Hilmi Veziroğlu (Bursa) 2.10.1980, Mehmet Cizreli (Mardin) 6.10.1980, Güldem Erdem (Ankara) 12.10.1980, Davut Elibolu (Adana) 29.10.1980, Şükrü Gedik (Gebze) 19.11.1980, Süleyman Ölmez (Tunceli) 16.11.1980, Yaşar Okçuoğlu (İstanbul) 4.12.1980, Mehmet Dağ (Adana) 29.12.1980, Munzur Geçgel (İzmir) 12.1980, Mustafa Şabin (Elazığ) 1.1.1981, Mehmet Ali Kılıç (Ankara) 12.2.1981, Ünsal Beydoğan (İstanbul) 25.2.1981, Sabri Kandemir (Kayseri) 5.3.1981, Cemil Kıpırdamaz (Uşak) 10.3.1981, Abdullah Peksoylu (Adıyaman) 16.3.1981, Şahin Satılmış Dokuyucu (Ankara) 18.3.1981, Osman Karaduman (İzmir/Ada ı) 20.3.1981, Hasan Gazioğlu (İstanbul) 30.3.1981, Necip Kutlu (Konya) 8.4.1981, Ahmet Sakin, Süleyman Cihan (İstanbul)

30.7.1981, Bayram Kocabaş (Ankara) 21.8.1981, Mehmet Yıldız (Ankara) 13.9.1981, İsmail Esen (Bursa) 15.11.1981, Önder Demirok 3.1981, Coşkun Altun (İstanbul) 16.6.1982, Ali Özbey (Diyarbakır) 23.8.1982, Jones Rumpf (Bursa) 23.9.1982, Behçet Dinlerer (Ankara) 15.12.1980, Niyazi Gündoğdu (Sivas) 16.3.1983, Hüsnü Seyhan (Ankara) 23.9.1983, Necmettin Büyükada (Diyarbakır) 18.7.1984, Kemal Gezgin (Ankara) 3.1985, Hasan Akan (Şırnak) 14.4.1985, Vedat Aldoğan (Ankara) 17.5.1985, Haydar Öztürk (Ankara) 29.5.1985, İbrahim Polat (Mardin) 28.9.1985, Kenan Özcan (Fatsa) 20.10.1985, Yaşar Durmaz (Samsun) 9.2.1986, Ömer Çavuşoğlu (Ankara) 28.5.1986, Yusuf Alta (Pazarcık)

DEAD DURING INTERROGATION

Mustafa Çevik (Trabzon) 17.9.1986, Zeki Yumurtacı (İstanbul) 17.9.1980, Ramazan Oğuz (Antalya) 20.9.1980, Hasan Dönmez (İstanbul) 2.10.1980, Cavit Özer (İstanbul) 2.10.1980, Emin Alkan (Siirt) 4.10.1980, Fuat Gürbüz (Malatya) 6.11.1980, Feridun Yılmaz (Eskişehir) 11.12.1980, İbrahim Eski (Ankara) 14.11.1980, Rüstem Gürsoy (İstanbul) 14.11.1980, Mehmet Samı (İstanbul) 6.12.1980, Cengiz ..... (Sivas) 16.12.1980, Engin İloke (Ankara) 16.12.1980, Mahmut Kaya (Erzurum) 25.12.1980, Mahmut ..... 27.12.1980, Nihat Ardu (Ankara) 1.1.1981, Hakan Mermeroğlu (İstanbul) 3.1.1981, Şerif Sar (Ankara) 3.1.1981, İlyas Güleç (İstanbul) 6.1.1981, Adil Ali Yılmaz (Ankara) 16.1.1981, Hasan Kekçe (Tunceli) 1.1980, Mehmet Emin Kutlu ..... 12.2.1981, Hayrettin Eren 2.1981, Mehmet Ali Erhay (Adıyaman) 16.3.1981, Turhan Sağlam (Kars) 3.1981, Şadiye Yavuz (Manisa) 1.4.1981, Aziz Ağaç (Adana) 3.4.1981, Özalp Öner (İstanbul) 4.5.1981, Selim Martin, Mehmet

Gümüş (Giresun) 5.1981, Mustafa Kılıç 8.7.1981, Yakup Göktaş (İstanbul) 27.7.1981, Aynur ..... (Uşak) 8.1981, Metin Serthulut (İzmir) 10.1981, Ali Altıok 1981, Mehmet Bağdaş 1981, İsmail Çelik (İstanbul) 2.1.1982, Mustafa Tunç (İstanbul) 1.1982, Abdurrahman Aksoy (Samsun) 1.1981, Şerif Yaz 1.1981, Ahmet Erdoğdu (Ankara) 10.2.1982, Süleyman Şeker (Bozova) 2.1981, Cennet Coçuman 3.1982, Abdülkadir Kaya 20.7.1985, Şehmuz Babuş 20.7.1982, Adnan Zincirkıran (Urfa) 9.1982, Gazel ..... 10.1982, Mustafa ..... 10.1982, Hasan Sertkaya 10.1982, Aziz Ertaş (Urfa/Halfeti) 12.1982, Fehmi Ozarslan (Ankara) 1982, İsmet Taş (İstanbul) 1982, M. Muthu Çetin (Manisa) 1.1983, Zekeriya Erdoğan (Ankara) 24.2.1983, Sevgi Kılıç 2.1984, Hüseyin Aydın (İstanbul) 7.1985, Zekeriya Ulkücü (İstanbul) 14.2.1986, Ayhan Alar, Hasan Akmoğlu.

DEAD IN PRISON

Reku Reş (Ankara) 12.11.1980, Sedat Özkaracadağ (Adana) 4.1.1981, Abdurrahman Çarkin 4.5.1984, Cemal Arat (Diyarbakır) 17.6.1984, Abdullah Meral (İstanbul) 15.6.1984, Fatih Öktülmüş (İstanbul) 17.6.1984, Hasan Telci (İstanbul) 26.6.1984, Haydar Başbağ (İstanbul) 5.1984, Adil Can (İstanbul) 15.4.1985, Kazım Çakır (Mersin) 7.6.1985, Halil Vasik (Fethiye) 17.9.1985, Serumah Kanzu (Çanakkale) 9.1985, Hasan Hüseyin Erbil (Uşak) 3.3.1986, Akif Yılmaz (Diyarbakır) 4.11.1982, Döndü ..... 1982.

SHOT DEAD

Hüseyin Karakuş (İskenderun) 27.9.1980, Mehmet Selim Yücel 27.9.1980, Mehmet Selim Yücel (Mardin) 14.5.1981, Turgay Erhay (İstanbul) 24.10.1982, Aziz Büyükertaş (Diyarbakır) 22.12.1982, Mustafa Tepeli (İstanbul) 1982, Mehmet Akpınar (Diyarbakır) 25.1.1983, Medet Özbadem (Diyarbakır) 20.5.1983, Yılmaz Demir (Diyarbakır) 20.1.1984, Remzi Astürk (Diyarbakır) 20.1.1984, Hüseyin Yüce (Diyarbakır) 1984.

DISAPPEARED

Ergin Şen (Bursa) 13.9.1980, Halil Gündoğan (İstanbul) 9.1980, Sait Şimşek 9.1980, Ahmet Altun, Cumali Ay, Atalay Bahadırlı, Günay Balçık, Bedri Bilge, Benli Coşkun (Nizip), Halil Çınar, Hüseyin Çolak, Kemal Demel, Aydın Demirkol, Şehmuz Durgun, Battal Evren, Sait Gözel, Mehmet Ali Karasoy, Mehmet Kazgan, İsmail Kıran, Gürkan Müngan, İsmet Omurcan, Yıldırım Özkan, Dursun Özkan, Dede Oğuzhan, Sermet Parkın, Yılmaz Pekör, Teoman Sezmanlı, Şerafettin Tınç, Taner Uzun, Bahar Yıldız, Resime ....., İsa ......, Gürabet Demirel (Diyarbakır) 21.3.1982, Mehmet Direrci (Diyarbakır), 21.3.1982 Mazlum Doğan (Diyarbakır), 21.3.1982 Mehmet Ali ..... (Diyarbakır), 21.3.1982, Şahan ..... (Diyarbakır), 21.3.1982, M. Ali Eraslan (Diyarbakır), 21.3.1982, Ali Erek (Diyarbakır) 21.3.1982, Cemal Kılıç (Diyarbakır), 21.3.1982, Cemal Zengin (Diyarbakır), 21.3.1982 Mahmut Zengin (Diyarbakır), 21.3.1982, Ferhat Kurtan (Diyarbakır), 21.3.1982, Eşref Milli (Diyarbakır), 21.3.1982, Necmi Öner (Diyarbakır), 21.3.1982 Tahir Şahin (Diyarbakır), 21.3.1982, Bedil Tan (Diyarbakır), 21.3.1982, Resmi Yalvaç 2.1981, Halil Ulni, Hasan ..... 27.12.1980, Bahadır Durmanlı (İstanbul), Ramazan Yayan, Arif Coşkun (Ankara), 3.7.1984, Sırrı Çıpur, Gülşah Teke, Hasan Akar (Bozova).

149

APPENDIX 4

Secret

TURKISH REPUBLIC

Chief of Staff

Martial Law Command of the provinces
of Diyarbakir, Hakkari, Mardin, Siirt,
Urfa and Van
                           DIYARBAKIR
SYNT: 7130-1299-82/1SHT.1835

                          16 July 1982

Subject: Use of Kurdish in government offices
To the
Deputy Martial Law Command
DIYARBAKIR

1. The Martial Law Command has learnt by way of various questions
   and inquiries that some officials and employees are continuing
   to speak Kurdish in certain government offices in this region
   and to accept and answer oral inquiries in this language.

2. The official language of the State is Turkish and no other
   language may be used in any government authority.

3. A person who by tolerating the use of the Kurdish language in
   government offices makes himself into a tool of the separatist
   ambitions of those who seek to split the unity of the Turkish
   nation and participates in such conversations which must at the
   very least be considered acts of provocation, and who does not
   cease such activity shall be prosecuted under Martial Law Regulation No. 1402.

4. The appropriate authorities who have the prime responsibility
   for carrying out these instructions shall be held responsible
   during checks and investigations by the Martial Law Command.

I request you to bring this order to the attention of the competent
authorities and to make the necessary arrangements.

KEMAL YAMAK
General Commanding the 7th Army
and Martial Law Commander
(copy certified identical with the original)
   signature

150

APPENDIX 5

The Turkish Republic
The Lord Major of Diyarbakir

July 8, 1981

Interoffice Memo: 45

Reference: the language spoken.

1. This highest office has received reports that employees
   and workers have spoken Kurdish in different departments
   as well as in the corridors of the main building.
2. I choose not to believe that such conversations have taken
   place.
3. Consistent action will be taken against those employees
   and workers when I have ascertained that they speak Kurdish
   instead of TURKISH at work.
4. Since we live as Turkish citizens we must speak Turkish. I
   repeat again explicitly, when it has been ascertained that
   employees and workers speak Kurdish in the offices and
   corridors at work, the appropriate legal action will be
   taken immediately against them and, also, against the department head.
5. This order will be read to, and signed by, all personal..
   A copy with signatures must be sent to the chairmen.

Please take note.

Sent: to all acting department chairmen.

Signature
Feyyaz Üzümcü
Military police-first lieutenant
Lord Major

APPENDIX 6

"It has been ascertained that folk dances known as 'Asiret dances' are being presented to the people of East and South-East Anatolia for ethnic and separatist purposes; it has further been ascertained that the songs sung during performances of these dances are in a language other than Turkish. This situation must be considered as damaging to our national unity and integrity. The necessary measures must be taken to ensure that the songs accompanying these folk dances are sung in no other language."

Hasan Saglam, Minister for National Education of the Republic of Turkey, to all Provincial Governors. *Cumhuriyet*, December 11, 1982.

APPENDIX 7

Verdict

File number: 1981/35
Resolution number: 1983/61
Judge: Namine Kilic, 25220
Plaintiff: Public Law
Accused: Ali Ekrem Kutlay, son of Süleyman, born in Agri,
                    registered in Leylekpınar Mahallesi, residence
                    in Lise Lojmanlari - Agri

                    Registry Office of Agri

Charge: Emendation of a Name
Date: February 2, 1981
Resolution date: May 6, 1983

The proceedings of 1981/2 were brought before this court in response
to the charges (#1979/108) prepared by the government prosecutor's
office.

The following judgement has been reached:

In the name of the plaintiff, the government prosecutor, this trail
was openned against Ali Ekrem Kutlay and against the Registry Office
in Agri with the purpose of the emendation of a name.

The first names of Ali Ekrem Kutlay's children do not correspond to
the record regulations as stated in Article 77. The children are
registered at the Registry Office in Leylekpinar,.Agri, in volume
number: 013, page 17,register 11. The son, Brusk Kutlay, born on
June 16, 1874, is in the third grade in elementary school. The
daughter is Bineos Kutlay, born on July 17, 1976.

The names Brusk and Bineos are contradictory to good morals, damage
the national cultur and tradition, and affect the interests of the
Turkish Republic.

Therefore, in regard to the documents of the Registry Office from
the 19th of October, 1979,file number 5533; as a result of this tria
the names should be emended, with every consideration taken for the
possible damages that could arise from the publicity.
With every consideration taken for the possible damages that could
arise from the publicity, the government prosecutor will record this
judgement in the indictment. The Registry Office will seize the
accused's family records book and will add the proper information.

The accused, Ali Ekrem Kutlay, whose statement has been submitted
before us, stated:
The names Brusk and Bineos were chosen by a friend. When the names
were registered the Registry Office raised no protest. There were
no bad intentions in the choice of these names. The children are
called by these names by friends and acquaintences as well as in
public. With a name change the children will suffer from identity
problems. Thus, the children could be called Mehmet-Brusk and Emine
Bineos. He stated further that the names are not contradictory to
good morals.

The public prosecutor, Hasan Yilmaz, the plaintiff's representative
for public law, proposed that the name Brusk Kutlay be changed to
Mehmet and that the name Bineos Kutlay be changed to Emine.

The accused Registry Office responded, that an emendation of the
accused's childrens names to Mehmet and Emine would not go against
the regulations of the Registry Office.

After statements from the parties present and the review of the file
the following judgement has been reached:
Since the names Brusk and Bineos go against the national cultur,
tradition, and morals, the children of the accused, Ali Ekrem Kutlay
(also responsible for the upbringing), will be called Mehmet and
Emine.

154

This judgement was issued for the above named reasons.

Verdict: for the above named reasons.

The first name of Brusk Kutlay, born to Nesrin on June 16, 1974, son of Ali Ekrem Kutlay, registered in Agri Tayyare Mahallesi, volume 13, page 17, register number 11, will be deleted and to Mehmet Kutlay emended. At the same time, the first name of Bineos Kutlay, born to Nesrin on July 17, 1976, daughter of Ali Ekrem Kutlay, will be deleted and to Emine Kutlay emended. This will also be so registered at the Registry Office. The facts and proceedings will be publicized in the local public proceedings notice.

Since this trial affects the interests of publicity, the costs of the trial will be born by the state, whose representative works in the interest of the government prosecutor's publicity.

The judgement was pronounced in the presence of the accused, Ali Ekrem Kutlay, the defendant from the Registry Office, and the plaintiff's representative, public prosecutor Hasan Yilmaz.

Appeals will not be allowed.

Recorder of the Minutes   Judge

Signature   Signature, Stamp

APPENDIX 8

Translation

T.R.

Ministry of Agriculture, Forestry and Village Works
General Directorate of Forestry

No. KDM-3, 5878-639-2418
Subject: Villages to be re-settled
Ankara
December 22, 1986

REGIONAL DIRECTORATE OF FORESTRY - ELAZIG

Articles 169 and 170 of our Constitution provide that forest areas may be taken out of the forestry borders, opened to agriculture and improved by the State, and that inhabitants of forest villages may be resettled.

During 1987, according to Forestry Law 6831, Article 2/A, while the process of taking some forest areas out of the forestry borders has started, similarly, according to Forestry Law Article no. 13/B, there is a need to determine the inhabitants who will be resettled from those areas and the inhabitants who voluntarily wish to be resettled.

Implementation decree no. 2924 (the law related to the support of the development of forest peasants) is published in the Official Gazette dated January 6, 1986, no. 1890, and put into effect.

According to Article 2/A of Forestry Law 6831, those areas which are going to be taken out of the forestry borders may generally be in or around areas such as Mersin-Antalya- Mugla-Izmir whose soil productivity is high. These areas will be improved and reconstructed by the State; housing, schools, mosques and other social buildings will be provided by the State and each household will be given a sufficient amount of land for agriculture. The houses and land in the villages of the people who will be resettled there will be turned into forests. (Law No. 2924)

Forming the basis of our work in the year 1987, according to Article 13/B of Forestry Law 6831, I would like to ask you to prepare separate reports for each village that needs to be transported and send them to the Center; also to complete the necessary studies and research in your region in order to provide information as to the village inhabitants who wish to be re- settled individually or collectively, and send this information to the Center within two months.

Mehmet Ali Karadeniz
General Director
Sign.

156

Ministry of Agriculture, Forestry and Village Works
GENERAL DIRECTORATE OF FORESTRY - ELAZIG
REGIONAL DIRECTORATE OF FORESTRY

Elazig
December 29, 1986

Part: Kd.
H. No.: Kd. 30
U. No.: 13451
Subject: Villages to be re-settled

DIRECTORATE OF FOREST WORKS - TUNCELI

The above is true copy of the orders of our general directorate. In order to perform the necessary studies and research within your region, a Commission is established, to be headed by Kamil Mazlum, regional vice directorate, Resat Ozenci, Branch Director of Operations and your Chief of Operations.

For your information.

Sign.
Regional Director
Sahin CAVULDAK
Regional Director of Forestry

Deliver to:

Kamil MAZLUM
Resat OZENCI
8 Directorates of Operations

SOURCES

Amnesty International, London; Chicago *Tribune*; *The Christian Science Monitor*, Boston; *Cumhuriyet*, Istanbul; *The Economist*, London; *The Financial Times*, London; Foreign Broadcast Information Service; *The Guardian*, London; Helsinki Watch, *Freedom and Fear: Human Rights in Turkey*; *Hurriyet*, Istanbul; *Info-Turk*, Brussels; International Helsinki Federation for Human Rights, *Turkey: Torture and Political Prisoners*, Vienna; *Milliyet*, Istanbul, *The New York Times*, *Newsweek*, New York; *Nokta*, Istanbul; *Oguzluge*, Marburg; PEN American Center, New York; *Tercuman*, Istanbul; *Turkey Briefing*, London; *Turkish Daily News*, Ankara; *Yeni Gundem*, Istanbul; *The Wall Street Journal*, New York; *2000'e Dogru*, Istanbul.

RECENT PUBLICATIONS FROM HELSINKI WATCH

Afghanistan:
To Win the Children: Afghanistan's Other War, December 1986, 21 pages. Photographs. $10.00.
To Die in Afghanistan, December 1985, 105 pages. $8.00.

Bulgaria:
Destroying Ethnic Identity: The Turks of Bulgaria -- An Update, September 1987, 58 pages. $6.00.
Violations of the Helsinki Accords: Bulgaria, November 1986, 33 pages. $5.00.
Destroying Ethnic Identity: The Turks of Bulgaria, June 1986, 39 pages. $6.00.

Czechoslovakia:
A Decade of Dedication: Charter 77, 1977-1987, January 1987, 97 pages. $8.00.
Violations of the Helsinki Accords: Czechoslovakia, November 1986, 41 pages. $6.00.

East Germany:
Violations of the Helsinki Accords: East Germany, November 1986, 41 pages. $6.00.

Hungary:
Violations of the Helsinki Accords: Hungary, November 1986, 40 pages, $6.00.

Poland:
Reinventing Civil Society: Poland's Quiet Revolution 1981-1986, December 1986, 101 pages. $8.00.
Violations of the Helsinki Accords: Poland, November 1986, 84 pages. $8.00.

Romania:
Violations of the Helsinki Accords: Romania, November 1986, 47 pages. $6.00.

Turkey:
State of Flux: Human Rights in Turkey, December 1987, 157 pages. $8.00.
Violations of the Helsinki Accords: Turkey, November 1986, 91 pages. $8.00.
Freedom and Fear: Human Rights in Turkey, March 1986, 122 pages. $6.00.

USSR:

Violations of the Helsinki Accords: Soviet Union, November 1986, 343 pages. $12.00.
U.S. Broadcasting to the Soviet Union, September 1986, 135 pages. $10.00.
The Moscow Helsinki Monitors: Their Vision, Their Achievement, The Price They Paid; May 12, 1976-May 12, 1986, May 1986, 60 pages. $5.00.

Yugoslavia:
Violations of the Helsinki Accords: Yugoslavia, November 1986, 91 pages. $6.00.

General Publications:
From Below: Independent Peace and Environmental Movements in Eastern Europe and the USSR, October 1987, 263 pages. $12.00.
Violations of the Helsinki Accords, November 1986, 9 reports, full set. $40.00
Mother of Exiles: Refugees Imprisoned in America, June 1986, 59 pages. Photographs. $8.00.
Ten Years Later: Violations of the Helsinki Accords, August 1985, 329 pages. $10.00.